THE IMPACTS OF 9/11 ON CANADA–U.S. TRADE

The events of 9/11 and subsequent border entry security initiatives have led to increased costs and transportation delays that have the potential to impact Canada–U.S. trade. Researchers have identified increased border crossing times for importers and exporters transporting goods between the two countries, but there has been little effort made to identify the quantitative importance of these developments in terms of their effect on bilateral trade flows. In this study, Steven Globerman and Paul Storer fill this gap in the existing research through statistical analysis of trade flows since 9/11.

Among the questions undertaken in this book are whether trade flows are lower in the post-9/11 period than they might otherwise have been, and whether factors apart from 9/11 influenced trade in major bilateral sectors. Globerman and Storer show that U.S. exports to Canada decreased significantly in the aftermath of 9/11, although such exports had recovered by 2004. In contrast, while U.S. imports from Canada also suffered a significant post-9/11 decrease, a shortfall between actual and expected imports from Canada persisted through 2005. In other words, by mid-2005 Canadian exports to the U.S. had not regained their 'normal' level. These and other conclusions are crucial to understanding the impact that increased border security has had on the economic relationship between Canada and the United States.

STEVEN GLOBERMAN is Kaiser Professor of International Business at Western Washington University.

PAUL STORER is an associate professor in the College of Business and Economics at Western Washington University.

STEVEN GLOBERMAN
PAUL STORER

The Impacts of 9/11 on Canada–U.S. Trade

UNIVERSITY OF TORONTO PRESS
Toronto Buffalo London

© University of Toronto Press Incorporated 2008
Toronto Buffalo London
www.utppublishing.com
Printed in Canada

ISBN 978-0-8020-9786-6

Printed on acid-free paper

Library and Archives Canada Cataloguing in Publication

Globerman, Steven
    The impact of 9/11 on Canada-U.S. trade / Steven Globerman, Paul Storer.

    Includes bibliographical references and index.
    ISBN 978-0-8020-9786-6

    1. September 11 Terrorist Attacks, 2001 – Economic aspects – Canada – Statistics.   2. September 11 Terrorist Attacks, 2001 – Economic aspects – United States – Statistics.   3. Canada – Commerce – United States.   4. United States – Commerce – Canada.   I. Storer, Paul.   II. Title.

    HF3228.U3G56 2008   382.0971073'0021   C2007-906838-3

University of Toronto Press acknowledges the financial assistance to its publishing program of the Canada Council for the Arts and the Ontario Arts Council.

University of Toronto Press acknowledges the financial support for its publishing activities of the Government of Canada through the Book Publishing Industry Development Program (BPIDP).

To our families
Daryl, Evan, and Martine
Tina, Leah, and Nick

Contents

Preface

This study is part of a longer-run commitment on the authors' part to understand better the forces that are shaping North American economic and political integration, particularly between Canada and the United States. Our commitment is built upon more than academic interest. Both of us have lived and worked for long periods of time in each country, and we have family and friends on both sides of the border. A thriving and prosperous partnership between Canada and the United States is of deep personal concern to us.

The terrorist attacks on the United States that took place on 11 September 2001 brought about profound geopolitical and economic changes affecting the entire world. From an economic perspective, the immediate changes were perhaps most visible in the temporary closing of the world's longest, hitherto undefended border. For several anxious days, personal vehicle and commercial traffic flowing between the two countries was disrupted – a momentous disturbance to the largest bilateral trading relationship in the world. Politicians and bureaucrats on both sides of the border quickly acknowledged the critical necessity of reopening the border under conditions that promised both security and relatively unrestricted ease of crossing for both commercial and personal travellers. Bilateral agreements and programs to promote such a regime have followed, and the monumental chaos that characterized the reopening of border crossings in the aftermath of 9/11 is, fortunately, a memory. Nevertheless, many North American managers argue that border crossing conditions for commercial traffic remain 'more difficult' than in the pre-9/11 period and that those conditions are a lingering and significant deterrent to closer economic integration between the two countries.

The creation of the Border Policy Research Institute (BPRI) at Western Washington University in 2005 was the immediate catalyst for this study. In particular, the director of the BPRI, Professor Don Alper, was enthusiastic about our studying the effects of post-9/11 border security initiatives on Canada–U.S. trade, and his institute provided generous funding that afforded us the time to research and write this study, as well as to hire research assistants and purchase data and other supplies. In fact, one of the authors had undertaken some earlier research on the responses of multinational companies to border disruptions post-9/11 for the Government of Canada. This earlier research facilitated our proposal for a larger and more ambitious research project funded by the BPRI.

We are indebted to numerous individuals who lent their talents, in one way or another, to our efforts. As noted, Don Alper helped us secure funding and continues to inspire our commitment to researching and writing about the bilateral relationship. Jame Donovan was a research assistant nonpareil. He created a large and complex electronic database that enabled us to extract statistical information and econometric estimation results both quickly and accurately. Equally important, he kept us alert and honest to our task by asking critical questions about the data we were collecting and the econometric models we were asking him to run. The comments of two unidentified reviewers also resulted in substantial improvements to the original draft.

Jim Pettinger supplied information and practical insights into the actual business of shipping goods across the border, and Judith Appleby and Rochelle Sandeen provided technical and word processing support in a cheerful and efficient manner. Stefan Freelan helped with the creation of maps. The study was supported by the U.S. Department of Transportation, Office of the Secretary, Grant No. DT0S59-05-G-0016

THE IMPACTS OF 9/11 ON CANADA–U.S. TRADE

1 Introduction

At 8:47 a.m. on 11 September 2001, American Airlines Flight 11 crashed into the north side of the North Tower of the World Trade Center in New York City after it was hijacked by terrorists. At 9:03 a.m. local time, United Airlines Flight 175 crashed into the South Tower of the World Trade Center. At around 9:38 a.m., a third hijacked airplane, American Airlines Flight 77, smashed into the Pentagon in Washington, D.C. A fourth hijacked aircraft crashed in a field in Somerset County, Pennsylvania, at 10:03 a.m. after a group of passengers attempted by force to regain control of the airplane from terrorists. Later that morning, both towers of the World Trade Center, as well as surrounding buildings, collapsed, with a loss of life in the thousands.

Immediately after the 9/11 attacks, the United States closed its airports, seaports, and land crossings with both Canada and Mexico. When the borders reopened days later, U.S. Customs officials began subjecting commercial traffic and personal travellers entering the United States to intensive inspections that, among other things, delayed truck carriers for up to eighteen hours. Hence, while the terrorist attacks themselves had been launched at the United States, the economic and political shockwaves of those attacks swept through Canada, as the world's largest bilateral trading relationship effectively shut down. Unfounded rumours that several of the hijackers had entered the United States from Canada intensified concerns among influential American politicians that Canada's 'lax' immigration and domestic security arrangements had made the world's longest undefended border a direct security threat to the United States. These concerns had been encouraged several years earlier by the arrest of a Canadian citizen of North African origin when he attempted to cross the border from Canada into the United States with explosives in his automobile and with the intention of setting off explosions at Los Angeles International Airport.

For several tense days following 9/11, the future of the world's longest undefended political border was surrounded by uncertainty. However, it quickly became clear that the high degree of economic integration between the two countries would be seriously compromised – with disastrous economic consequences for both countries – unless the ability of commercial shippers to cross the border was restored to something approximating pre-9/11 conditions. At the time of the 9/11 attacks, around 500,000 people and 50,000 trucks crossed between Canada and the United States every day (Bissett 2003). Ensuring that this traffic could continue to cross relatively expeditiously while meeting the heightened need to block future terrorist attacks posed a major public policy challenge in the short and long run. As a practical political matter, new initiatives were necessary to restore confidence – particularly among many U.S. government representatives – that the dual objectives of facilitating trade and preserving domestic security could be realized insofar as they applied to the Canada–U.S. border.

Bilateral discussions at the highest political levels were initiated to try to ensure that the trade partnership between Canada and the United States did not suffer irreparable harm from the U.S. government's newly heightened focus on homeland security. While bilateral efforts to identify ways to ease congestion at northern border crossings had been ongoing prior to 9/11, developments in the aftermath of the tragedy created a sharp sense of urgency – particularly among Canadian politicians – to design and implement a new and cooperative risk-management regime at the Canada-U.S. border. The first major bilateral government initiative to emerge in the post-9/11 period was the Smart Border Program.

U.S.–Canada Smart Border Declaration

The Smart Border Declaration was signed by the two governments on 12 December 2001.[1] The declaration was a thirty-point plan organized into four categories: (1) the secure flow of people; (2) the secure flow of goods; (3) secure infrastructure; and (4) coordination and information sharing in support of the declaration's objectives. Perhaps the most prominent program as far as commercial shippers are concerned is the Free and Secure Trade (FAST) plan. FAST allows for the expedited border clearance of preapproved, low-risk commercial shipments across the Canada–U.S. border. Specifically, the FAST program offers importers, carriers, and drivers who qualify for the program joint and streamlined registration, expedited clearance at the border, and dedicated lanes. The anticipated benefits to shippers include these: (1) reduced the information requirements for customs clearance; (2) elimination of the need for importers to transmit data for each transaction; (3) dedicated lanes for FAST clearance; (4) reduction in the rate of border examinations; (5) verification of trade compliance away from the border; and (6) streamlined accounting and payment processes for all goods imported by approved importers (Canada only).

The FAST program is one of the two key measures taken by the U.S. government in the wake of 9/11. A second is the Customs-Trade Partnership Against Terrorism (C-TPAT). This is a joint government–business initiative to strengthen overall border and supply chain security. A business participating in C-TPAT must commit to specific actions; for example, it must develop and implement a program to enhance security throughout its supply chain in accordance with C-TPAT guidelines. The benefits of participating in the program include a reduced number of border inspections.

Three main participant groups are eligible for FAST – importers, carriers, and drivers. FAST is available to participants that can demonstrate a history of compliance with all relevant legislation and regulations and that have acceptable books, records, and audit trails. Since the fall of 2006, Canada and the United States have jointly offered expedited customs clearance processes to preauthorized drivers, carriers, and importers at twelve major border crossings, including[2] Lacolle, Quebec/Champlain, New York; Queenston, Ontario/Lewiston, New York; Fort Erie, Ontario/Buffalo, New York; Windsor, Ontario/Detroit, Michigan; Sarnia, Ontario/Port Huron, Michigan; and Pacific Highway, British Columbia/Blaine, Washington. The Lacolle/Champlain and Sarnia/Port Huron crossings have designated FAST lanes. Plans are for all major commercial crossings to be FAST capable in the future.

A number of specific programs covered by the Smart Border Declaration affect passenger vehicle crossings. Perhaps the most prominent is the NEXUS program, which has established dedicated lanes for low-risk travellers. Other initiatives included as part of the Smart Border

Program include these: the use of binational, multiagency border patrol and enforcement teams; increased information sharing regarding passengers bound for and departing from the United States; joint teams to ensure that all high-risk containers are examined when they arrive in North America (through the collection of advance manifest data for incoming ships and their containers; this is the Container Security Initiative); increased harmonization of visa policies; and the signing of a Statement of Mutual Understanding for information exchange on immigration-related issues.

The impacts of the Smart Border Program are matters for conjecture. In particular, strong controversy surrounds the social costs and benefits of the C-TPAT and FAST programs, as well as the Container Security Initiative. For example, the U.S. government has estimated that the requirement for transportation companies to alert the U.S. Bureau of Customs and Border Protection by computer or fax about the content and recipients of international cargo, either before it is loaded at a foreign port or before it reaches the United States, would cost less than $100 million. The U.S. government has also asserted that the required procedures will not slow down deliveries. On the other hand, some large manufacturers and transportation companies have argued that the changes will cost much more than $100 million and may well add to border crossing delays (Brooks 2003).

In terms of waiting times for shippers to cross the border, a relatively recent study of export shipments from Quebec to the United States concludes that commercial shippers complying with the C-TPAT/FAST security requirements for accelerated border clearance treatment experience wait times up to thirty minutes shorter than for shippers that do not comply.[3] At the same time, relatively low enrolment by shippers in the FAST Program provides potential support for concerns expressed that this program fails to provide significant net benefits to shippers in the way of cost savings.

Other Initiatives

Various other initiatives not directly related to the Smart Border Program have been undertaken in an effort to reduce average wait times and the variability of average wait times for commercial traffic crossing the northern border. They include improved road access to crossing facilities. For example, prior to improvements to the southbound access at the Pacific Highway/Blaine border crossing, even trucks enrolled in the expedited border crossing program (FAST) had to wait in line along with all the other trucks that had not precleared their cargo. The improved road access at the Pacific Highway/Blaine border crossing involved the design of a southbound commercial lane specifically designated for low-risk commercial vehicles, including FAST trucks. At the Blue Water Bridge between Sarnia and Port Huron, the typical number of booths to process shipments coming into the United States was increased from three to five in 2002.[4] It also became standard for booths to operate twenty-four hours per day. Battelle (2003) has estimated that this increased capacity was associated with a 10 per cent increase in truck traffic entering the United States in 2002–3. On the Ambassador Bridge connecting Windsor and Detroit, the privately owned Bridge Company put up funds to operate up to nine lanes at the primary U.S. checkpoints; there had been only six booths in the pre-9/11 environment.

Other approaches to mitigating border delays associated with increased security, besides improved facilities, include increased staffing and innovative methods to clear breakdowns and accidents from roadways that provide access to and from border crossings. For example, the provision of additional staff has been a priority on the Michigan side of the Blue Water and Ambassador Bridges. Since the number of booths open to process commercial traffic is a critical determinant of the speed with which commercial vehicles are cleared through border inspection procedures, we can assume that additional staffing has mitigated border congestion delays at those crossings.

The reorganization of the customs, immigration, and food inspection functions at the U.S. border has been credited by some observers with reducing the direct and indirect costs associated with commercial border crossings. On 2 September 2003, then Department of Homeland Security (DHS) Secretary Tom Ridge announced the 'One Face at the Border' initiative, which was designed to eliminate the previous separation of immigration, customs, and agricultural functions at all U.S. ports of entry in favour of a unified border inspection process. The plan created two broad new bureaux: the Bureau of Customs and Border Protection (CBP), which was created to handle border management, and the Bureau of Immigration and Customs Enforcement (ICE), which was created as the investigative arm of the directorate. CBP's was created to help meet the strategic goals of improving border security while, at the same time, facilitating the unimpeded and reliable flow of international commerce.[5]

A comparable reorganization was undertaken by the Canadian government in December 2003, with the creation of a new Ministry of Public Safety and Emergency Preparedness. The ministry includes a Canadian Border Services Agency (CBSA), which consolidates border functions previously spread among three organizations: the customs program of the Canada Revenue Agency; the Intelligence, Interdiction, and Enforcement Program of CIC; and the Import Inspection at Ports of Entry Program of the Canadian Food Inspection Agency. The CBSA completed its reorganization in October 2004 by transferring the immigration inspection functions at ports of entry from CIC to CBSA, comparable to locating U.S. immigration inspectors within DHS.

The Current Policy Environment

Notwithstanding the efforts undertaken by the Canadian and U.S. governments, as well as private-sector organizations, to reduce the delays and uncertainties surrounding border crossing conditions, a wide range of observers continue to express concern that border security issues are seriously damaging international trade between Canada and the United States.[6] Goldfarb (2005), among others, argues that the direct and indirect costs of current security procedures are disrupting the forces of economic integration between the two countries – forces that have been in place for decades. Lee and her colleagues (2005) assert that the delays and uncertainties occasioned by U.S. border security controls are a major concern for Quebec exporters and would-be exporters. The ongoing impact on bilateral trade of efforts to enhance border security is of obvious interest to policy makers, particularly in Canada, since over 80 per cent of Canada's exports are destined for the United States.

The Coalition for Secure and Trade-Efficient Borders (2005) asserts that, notwithstanding efforts by governments to balance imperatives for enhanced security with those for improved ease and reduced costs associated with border crossings, between 2002 and 2005 there was a significant increase in the introduction of regulatory initiatives and programs designed to protect the border by agencies in both Canada and the United States. The proliferation of initiatives and programs has increased the complexity of border processes; the result has been billions of dollars of compliance and delay costs at the border.[7]

A number of specific policy issues arise in the context of a possible continuing apparent trade-off between enhanced security against terrorism and increased bilateral trade and tourism.[8] One is a factual matter: What is the quantitative impact on trade and tourism of government responses to the perceived need for heightened border security in the post-9/11 era? While it might seem cavalier to suggest that North Americans generally, and Americans specifically, are paying too high a price for homeland security, particularly in the form of lower gains from trade with Canada than would otherwise be realized, the economic reality is that everything, including security, has a price. Indeed, the concept of 'risk management' that presumably underlies the Smart Border Declaration implicitly recognizes that specific contingencies may not be worth guarding against from a benefit–cost perspective.[9] Any evaluation of the benefits and costs of greater border security must therefore be informed by an identification of how bilateral trade is affected, since bilateral trade is widely accepted as providing substantial economic benefits to both countries.

If the adverse impacts of border security on bilateral trade are economically substantial, this strengthens policy arguments for spending more public funds on programs and infrastructure to expedite faster and more reliable border crossings by commercial shippers.[10] To the extent that adverse impacts of border delays are disproportionately experienced by one or the other trading partner, the associated policy implications are more problematic. In particular, governments tend to worry more about disruptions to exports from their country than about disruptions to imports into their country. While this mercantilist assessment of trade is misguided and lamentable, it may well be a political reality. In this regard, there is a widespread perception that U.S. policymakers are less concerned than their Canadian counterparts with expediting trade, especially if doing so entails any significant perceived sacrifice of security against terrorism. Had Canada's exports to the U.S. been adversely affected by post-9/11 border security developments, whereas U.S. exports to Canada had not, the prospects of enthusiastic bilateral efforts to address border-related trade disruptions would arguably be much weaker than if exports from both countries had been affected. Evidence bearing on the impacts of post-9/11 developments on trade flows may therefore be of particular interest to Canadian policy makers in helping them to better understand the bilateral bargaining environment in which they are operating.

Also useful to policy makers is information about whether the impact of post-9/11 developments on trade has been widespread or whether it has focused largely on specific commodities and/or specific border crossings. It is certainly possible that the impacts of border-crossing delays and uncertainties have been disproportionately experienced by specific shippers. For example, Goldfarb and Robson (2003) outline a set of reasons for expecting certain commodities to be more affected by increased border security procedures than others, and we will discuss their criteria in more detail in a later section. Also, since individual border crossings differ regarding the mix of goods that are brought through by shippers, border crossing conditions may well vary by port location, depending on a specific port's commodity mix as well as the physical infrastructure and staffing levels characterizing that port.

In the context of limited public-sector financing, it would make sense to give funding priorities to initiatives that promise the largest benefits in terms of alleviating barriers to cross-border flows of goods and people. This could mean concentrating public-sector initiatives on specific border crossing locations or on specific modes of transportation. It might also highlight sectors of the economy where consultation and policy coordination between the public and the private sector are likely to do the most to mitigate border disruptions. Knowledge of the extent to which adverse impacts on trade are concentrated at specific locations is of obvious value in setting funding priorities.

Finally, knowledge of how border crossing activities are being affected by security arrangements is of basic interest to planners at both the state/provincial and local levels of government, particularly as it affects decisions regarding public investments in transportation infrastructure. In border communities such as Whatcom County in Washington State, highway traffic is very sensitive to changes in the volume of goods shipped along the I-5 corridor that originate or terminate in British Columbia's Lower Mainland. To the extent that the long-run trajectory of this traffic is likely to be affected by border security initiatives, the net benefits of alternative transportation infrastructure expansion plans will also be affected.

This study proceeds as follows. Chapter 2 places this study in context by describing the nature of the border in terms of physical geography, infrastructure, and border security policy, such as a perimeter security approach. A combination of descriptions, maps, and tables is used to identify the location of crossing points along the physical border. Next, border concerns are surveyed with an emphasis on the counter-terrorism focus that has emerged in the United States in the aftermath of 9/11.

Chapter 3 provides an overview of bilateral trade in goods. Specifically, it describes the bilateral trade process in terms of the volume and composition of bilateral trade pre- and post-9/11, the largest land ports along the Canada–U.S. border, and the main modes of transporting goods between the two countries. Finally, it identifies the types of goods that are most economically vulnerable to security-related border disruptions.

Chapter 4 reviews available studies of the impacts of increased border security on bilateral trade flows. One set of studies provides 'snapshot' estimates of waiting times at border crossings that highlight the existence of border crossing delays, particularly for commercial shipments crossing into the United States from Canada. A second set reports estimates of the added financial costs of border congestion and associated delays in shipments crossing the border. A third offers some partial or indirect assessments of the impacts of post-9/11 border developments on total border crossings by carriers and on overall trade volumes. The various studies suggest that substantial added costs and uncertainties were imposed on commercial shippers in the immediate aftermath of 9/11. Notwithstanding efforts by the two governments to mitigate these adverse impacts, it appears that border delays and uncertainties with respect to wait times are greater problems today than prior to 9/11; however, there is very little direct evidence relating to the consequences of these problems for bilateral trade flows. The limited evidence that indirectly bears on this issue is, at best, inconclusive. Specifically, while the evidence points towards the likelihood of lingering adverse impacts on trade, it fails to document the severity of those impacts.

Chapter 5 sets out the methodology underlying the empirical analysis. Specifically, it describes a parsimonious statistical model of U.S. trade with Canada spanning a time period from the first quarter of 1996 through the second quarter of 2001. U.S. export and import equations (with Canada) are specified, with the independent variables drawn from previous studies of international trade determinants. The chapter discusses how the impacts of 9/11 are estimated using time dummy variables, which are added to the basic export and import equations, which are 'calibrated' using pre-9/11 data. Issues arising from our approach, as well as caveats concerning the interpretation of our statistical findings, are also discussed.

Chapter 6 describes our estimation of basic export and import equations; these in turn are used to identify the impacts of 9/11 on bilateral trade. Aggregate export and import equations are initially estimated for quarterly periods prior to the third quarter of 2001. The estimated aggregate trade equations with gross domestic product (GDP), the Canada–U.S. exchange rate, and seasonal dummy variables as the independent variables are statistically robust, and the estimated regression coefficients are, for the most part, consistent with expectations based on economic theory.

To identify a potential '9/11 effect' over time, dummy variables are introduced into the basic trade equations estimated with pre-9/11 data. Specifically, dummy variables are specified to represent the third and fourth quarters of 2001, separately, the years 2002, 2003 and 2004, separately, and the first half of 2005. The trade equations are then re-estimated using data over the full sample period covering 1996 quarter one through 2005 quarter two. We find that adverse impacts on U.S. imports persist from the third quarter of 2001 through the second quarter of 2005, holding other conventional determinants of U.S. imports constant. Specifically, U.S. imports from Canada are around 12 per cent lower than they should have been based on conventional determinants of trade. We interpret this shortfall as a consequence of 9/11 border security–related impacts. Conversely, while U.S. exports to Canada are lower than they should have been based on conventional determinants of trade, the negative 9/11 impacts on U.S. exports disappear statistically by 2004. Thus, by 2004, U.S. exports are of a magnitude consistent with the basic trade model. We interpret this as evidence that the adverse effects of border security on U.S. exports had essentially disappeared by 2004.

Chapter 7 applies the statistical procedures discussed in chapter 6 to analyse developments at individual land ports. Specifically, we estimate the parsimonious equations identified in chapter 6 over the period 1996 quarter one through 2001 quarter two for the ten largest land ports of entry on the U.S. side of the border.[11] We then extend the basic export and import equations by adding post-9/11 time dummy variables specified in the same way as described in our summary of chapter 6. The basic trade equations including the time dummies are then re-estimated using data over the full period through 2005 quarter two.

With respect to U.S. imports from Canada, the overall pattern of the estimated coefficients for the time dummy variables is fairly similar across individual ports; however, there are clear differences across individual ports regarding the magnitudes of the estimated coefficients associated with each time period dummy variable. For example, U.S. imports from Canada entering through the Port of Detroit are actually higher in the first half of 2005 than would be expected based on conventional determinants of trade. At the other extreme, the Ports of Champlain–Rouses Point and Port Huron are characterized by substantially lower imports from Canada than would be expected.[12] Whereas all of the sample ports manifested a substantial reduction from expected levels for Canadian imports at some point in the post-9/11 period, only about half the major ports were still experiencing a significant negative impact by 2005. Substantial differences across ports are also identified with respect to U.S. exports to Canada. For example, while U.S. exports in 2005 are at expected levels for most sample ports, export levels for three major ports are below expected levels in 2005. In short, the security-related impacts on bilateral trade seem to differ across major ports.

Chapters 8 and 9 evaluate more fully the results reported in chapters 6 and 7. Specifically, in chapter 8, we consider the possibility that factors other than security-related border disruptions contributed to the observed 'shortfall' of U.S. imports from Canada in the post-9/11 period. One way we do so is by focusing on commodities that are primary exports from Canada to the U.S. but not from the U.S. to Canada. Since U.S. imports from Canada experienced the most substantial post-9/11 reductions from expected values, sources of explanation other than border security–related impacts must lie in experiences that are unique to Canadian export industries. As the data presented in chapter 3 indicate, autos and motor vehicles are major exports of both countries; however, oil and gas, and petroleum and forest products are major Canadian exports that are not substantial export products for the U.S. Hence, we explicitly consider whether other, non-security–related explanations might be relevant contributors to reductions in Canadian exports to the U.S. in these three industries in the post-9/11 period. We conclude that other post-9/11 developments potentially affecting major Canadian export industries are unlikely to be strong reasons for the statistical findings reported in chapter 6.

In chapter 9, we assess in more detail the port-level results discussed in chapter 7. Specifically, we consider possible explanations for port-level differences in post-9/11 trade flows. We are particularly interested in differences across U.S. ports of entry in terms of processing imports from Canada. The chapter first considers the possibility that commodity shipment differences across ports account for the observed differences in estimated 'shortfalls' of U.S. imports from Canada in the post-9/11 period. This possible explanation is rejected, in particular because of the differential experiences of ports for which motor vehicles are a major import category. We also explore the possibility that infrastructure, transport mode, and policy differences across ports might account for the estimated 9/11 impacts on Canadian imports for each port. While our assessment is speculative in the light of available evidence, we believe that such differences are likely to be of greater significance than differences in patterns of commodity shipments.

Chapter 10 considers the potential impacts of the estimated Canadian export shortfalls on capital investment in Canada. A particular concern of Canadians is that border disruptions will make Canada a less desirable location for production facilities. Our investigation of foreign and domestic capital investment in Canada bears on this issue.

Finally, a summary and set of policy recommendations are provided in chapter 11. In particular, alternative policy approaches to address the disruptive impact that post-9/11 security developments have had, and may have again in the future, are identified and discussed. Approaches towards bilateral cooperation figure prominently in this discussion. At the same time, the need for Canada to pursue independent initiatives that may indirectly affect U.S. government attitudes and policies towards cross-border transportation is also highlighted.

2 Security Policy and the Canada–U.S. Border

The path traced by the Canada–U.S. border is a product of history and politics that sometimes respects geographic realities but at others seems to ignore them. Whether the border is created by the St Lawrence River or by something as arbitrary as the 49th parallel, its existence has much the same implications for the flow of goods and people between Canada and the United States. For both countries, the border represents an access point to its largest trade partner, as well as to world trade more broadly since some foreign goods entering either country are transshipped to the other country. While both countries derive significant mutual benefits from cross-border trade, there have been times when each has viewed the border as a threat.

This study analyses the implications of the current U.S. focus on border security for the flows of trade between Canada and the United States. This section provides context for the study by surveying the geographic and administrative characteristics of the Canada–U.S. border. The nature of both legitimate and undesirable flows of goods and services is also discussed. The section concludes with a brief survey of policy options currently being considered to maintain the benefits of the border without exposing either country to undue security risks.

Geography of the Border

The total length of the Canada–U.S. border is 8891 km when the border running from the Atlantic to the Pacific is added to the border with Alaska. The portion from the Atlantic to the Pacific touches seven provinces and twelve states and is 6416 km long. The border with Alaska is 1538 km long and touches just one province and one Canadian territory. Slightly less than 57 per cent of the entire border (5061 km) runs on land; land accounts for just 45 per cent (2878 km) of the Atlantic–Pacific portion but 88 per cent (2183 km) of the border with Alaska.

The exact position of the border between Canada and the United States is determined by a series of line segments whose position is recorded by the International Boundary Commission (IBC), an institution jointly administered by the two countries. According to the website of the IBC,[1] the land border is identified by 5,528 physical boundary monuments that mark the beginning and end of each segment. There are also 5,723 unmarked 'turning points' for line segments on the water and 2,457 reference monuments. The various border treaties and agreements have created a few apparent anomalies, such as Point Roberts in Washington State and the northwest angle in Minnesota, small enclaves of U.S. territory whose only land connection to the rest of the United States passes through Canada. One of the tasks of the IBC is to maintain a partially cleared six-metre 'vista' to identify the boundary for the roughly 2000 km where it runs through forest or brush.

The bodies of water that form the border in the south of Canada vary from relatively small barriers, such as the St Croix River on the New Brunswick–Maine border, to the Great Lakes and the Strait of Juan de Fuca. The characteristics of the land border are equally varied. For example, in communities such as Rock Island (Stanstead) and Derby Line, the border divides a single Loyalist town between Quebec and Vermont. But there are also remote wilderness areas where the precise location of the border has little practical relevance.

These features of the border create several challenges. First, the manufacturing centres of Ontario and Quebec are located in the region of the country where water barriers are significant, either at the border itself (in the case of Ontario) or just north of the border (in the case of most of Quebec north of the St Lawrence). This explains why border crossings in this region tend to be concentrated at bridges or tunnels. In many cases, the portions of the border without water barriers are located relatively far from major manufacturing centres. The exception here is the northwest segment of Washington State and the Lower Mainland of British Columbia.

Border Inspection and Enforcement Infrastructure

The long border has created significant enforcement and inspection challenges. As of mid-2006, the Canada Border Services Agency (CBSA) listed 119 highway–land border offices located on the Canada–U.S. border.[2] The locations of the busiest Canadian offices, with the names of the corresponding U.S. border crossings, are shown on map 2.1.[3] The full set of Canadian crossings is provided by Tables 2.1a to 2.1g. The locations of the crossings are provided by the province-level maps 2.2a to 2.2j.[4]

Given that each crossing can cover only a limited section of the border, the sheer extent of the boundary means that long sections of the border have no official crossing point. While no part of the land border goes unmonitored, there are many places where remote sensing equipment must be used to detect unauthorized crossings, which results in slower reaction times when an intrusion is detected. In addition, both legitimate and clandestine water crossings by vessels can be made at numerous points along the lengthy water border, and small aircraft can cross the border at countless locations.

Concern with border security at points between official crossings is reflected in the Bush administration's Secure Border Initiative Net, which, since 2006, has devoted at least US$2.5 billion to improving security on the northern and southern borders of the U.S. Much of the spending has been for surveillance equipment such as drone aircraft. These investments augment previous approaches to bolstering border security, such as the stationing of Blackhawk helicopters at certain customs facilities along the northern border.

Ten of the 119 Canadian crossings do not allow commercial traffic to enter Canada. The remainder offer various levels of commercial services. As shown in Table 2.2, there are twenty-three Designated Commercial Offices, which operate twenty-four hours per day every day of the week. Ten of those are located in Ontario. All but three of the Designated Commercial Offices offer expedited clearance for commercial traffic enrolled in the Free and Secure Trade (FAST) program.

With one exception, each Canadian highway crossing is paired with a corresponding crossing that allows access to the U.S. by road.[5] The U.S. Census Bureau data used in this study are collected at the port-of-entry level, and smaller crossings are frequently grouped together to form a single port of entry. For example, the crossings between Woburn,

Quebec, and Coburn Gore, Maine, and between Ste-Aurélie, Quebec, and St Aurelie, Maine, are both part of the Jackman, Maine, port of entry. Most U.S. ports of entry are matched with a single Canadian highway crossing, but some ports of entry include as many as five Canadian crossings. As a result, while Canada lists 119 land crossings, the number of corresponding U.S. ports of entry on the Canada–U.S. border is only 77.[6]

While most of the cases of multiple combined Canadian crossings with a single U.S. port of entry occur at relatively isolated crossings, there are cases closer to population centres, such as the Buffalo–Niagara Falls port of entry (number 901), which includes four different Canadian crossings. Two of these crossings are the Rainbow and Whirlpool Bridges, which do not allow commercial traffic. The other two are the Queenston–Lewiston Bridge and the Peace Bridge in Fort Erie, both of which are Canadian Designated Commercial Offices. Tables 2.1 provide a full concordance between the U.S. port-of-entry designations and Canadian highway–land border offices.

Given that our focus is on the impact of border security on flows at the actual border, this study uses surface trade data only. In addition to road traffic, this includes shipments between Canada and the U.S. that pass by rail or by pipeline. Shipments by vessel or by air freight are not examined in this study because they are able to bypass the actual physical constraints at the border. In addition, air and water shipments typically do not occur at the same locations where passengers cross the border, and so potential security concerns differ between ports that handle trucks and trains and those that process airplanes and ships. We provide an overview of the nature of these security concerns in the next section.

Security and Trade and the Changing Focus at the Border

There has always been some ambivalence about the border on the part of both Canadians and Americans. Shortly after Canadian Confederation, campaign posters for Sir John A. Macdonald's National Policy showed images of wolf-like Americans who would devour the gentle folk of Canada if they were not kept at bay by the tariff 'wall.' Over time, the border has opened to the flow of goods and, to a lesser extent, to temporary workers who qualify under the terms of NAFTA (or the earlier Canada–U.S. Free Trade Agreement). Despite this, both countries have products and people deemed to be undesirable, and one of the main goals of border inspection and enforcement has been to prevent their entry.

The list of proscribed individuals and products is broadly similar for both Canada and the United States. The two countries prohibit the entry of illegal drugs, undocumented aliens, known criminals, articles made from endangered species, prohibited cultural artifacts, certain hateful or pornographic material, and public health threats. The visa requirements for third-country visitors are also broadly similar. There are also certain asymmetries, such as the U.S. embargo on trade with Cuba and Canada's ban on the entry of firearms and other potential weapons (such as pepper spray).

The focus of U.S. border security policy changed in the wake of 9/11. The Border Security website of the U.S. Customs and Border Protection Agency (CBPA) states that 'U.S. Customs and Border Protection's top priority is to keep terrorists and their weapons from entering the United States.'[7] Traditional security concerns such as narcotics and undocumented aliens remain important objectives, but the new priority is preventing the entry of potential terrorists as well as terror weapons such as conventional explosives, material for nuclear or radiological devices, and chemical or biological agents. Procedures for identifying terror suspects may differ from those used to identify conventional criminals or individuals engaged in smuggling drugs or people into the U.S.

The new approach to border security is summarized by the following statement from the 9/11 Commission Report (2004): 'The challenge for national security in an age of terrorism is to prevent the very few people who may pose overwhelming risks from entering or remaining in the United States undetected' (383). The report goes on to label the U.S. border and immigration system as a 'vital element of counterterrorism' (387).

The Canadian reaction to this new U.S. focus on securing the borders against terrorism has been broadly supportive, albeit with a certain undercurrent of irritation due to the costs imposed on Canadians visiting or doing business in the U.S. The position of the Martin government was summarized by Public Safety and Emergency Preparedness Minister Anne McLellan:

> Though the events of September 11, 2001, served as a catalyst in relation to our understanding of the need for a safe and secure border, our response has addressed a range of challenges that in fact had emerged earlier and will continue to evolve in the future. Terrorist threats, illegal migration, organized crime, and the introduction of previously unknown diseases,

such as SARS and the avian flu, all pose serious threats to our way of life. The CBSA's challenge is to protect Canadians while at the same time facilitating the flow of lawful people and trade, and it brings together the components necessary to meet this important goal. (McLellan 2005)

This statement by McLellan made the point that meeting the terrorist threat at the border partly involves continuing measures designed to counter previously existing security threats. To some extent, procedures implemented to prevent the entry of terrorists may complement efforts to block the flow of conventional criminals and illegal drugs. Equipment for detecting radioactive substances can presumably be installed in such a way that traffic is screened passively while in transit through the primary inspection post. On the other hand, there may be trade-offs if, for example, dogs trained to sniff explosives replace those previously used to detect drug smuggling. On a larger scale, given that it is not feasible to scrutinize each traveller and every shipment thoroughly for all conceivable threats, inspection priorities need to be set, and this could also impose a trade-off between security objectives.

The Canadian government has accepted the implications of the new U.S. priorities and has cooperated extensively in the implementation of new security measures. This has involved the commitment of additional resources, an increased level of collaboration, and enhanced sharing of information. At the same time, the Canadian government has taken pains to point out that none of the 9/11 terrorists entered the U.S. through Canada and that it was U.S. border screening procedures that were inadequate. Members of the Canadian public have sometimes been less diplomatic in pointing out this fact, particularly when reacting to the Western Hemisphere Travel Initiative, which will eventually require the use of secure identification for persons crossing the Canada–U.S. land border.

Canada did not provide 'back door' access to the U.S. for the 9/11 terrorists. This fact, however, has not been sufficient to calm U.S. concerns that possible terrorism threats might enter through Canada in the future. One reason for this is that the U.S. has recognized the inadequacies of its screening and monitoring procedures for aliens; presumably, this will lead to a hardening of the access points from non–North American locations. Without any corresponding changes in entry procedures that apply to Canada, the Canada–U.S. border would become a relatively more appealing access route for those wishing to inflict harm on the United States.

Other events have contributed to perceptions that the U.S. border with Canada must be subjected to a higher level of security. In December 1999, Ahmed Ressam, the 'Millennium Bomber,' was arrested as he tried to enter the U.S. on a ferry between Victoria, B.C., and Port Angeles, Washington. The blocking of this plot to bomb Los Angeles airport is a testimony to the vigilance of both Canadian and U.S. border enforcement personnel; nevertheless, it established the possibility that Canada could be used as an entry point for both terrorists and explosives. In June 2006 a number of arrests were made in an alleged domestic terror plot in the Toronto area. This plot apparently did not target the U.S.; nevertheless, it provided support to those who argue that Canada might be harbouring terrorists who are linked to (or at least sympathetic to) terrorist groups that do seek to harm the U.S.

Writing in the *Globe and Mail*, Koring (2006) noted that some U.S. politicians feared that 'lax security and the presence of a large Muslim population in Canada makes the country a natural staging ground for terrorist strikes.' The Canadian government and its representatives have made a strong effort to correct misconceptions about the security threat Canada poses to the U.S. – an effort that Koring characterized as an 'uphill battle.' Koring also quoted Carl Levin, a U.S. senator from the border state of Michigan, who observed that 'we have thousands of trucks that come in every day, many of them – most of them – not inspected. And particularly, by the way, garbage trucks from Ontario which cannot be inspected represent a real significant security threat.'

While the debate will continue regarding the validity of allegations that Canada is a security threat, there is no denying that some U.S policy makers view the Canada–U.S. border with suspicion. So it is probably inevitable that tightened security measures will remain in place at the border. As Ferrabee (2006) wrote in the *Toronto Star*, the 'U.S. may wrongly suspect Canada is soft on terrorists, but in the end it doesn't matter.' Given the clear U.S. emphasis on counterterrorism at the border, a realistic response for governments in Canada and for businesses and individuals on both sides of the border is to determine the best way to adapt to the new security environment. Our hope is that this study will aid in this process of adaptation by measuring the impact of increased security on trade at major U.S. ports of entry on the border with Canada.

Border Policy Responses and Issues

In the immediate aftermath of 9/11, all border crossings were closed and then gradually reopened with a significantly increased level of security. The severity of this response at the border reflected uncertainty regarding the precise nature and level of the terrorist threat and the need to evaluate and adapt to the new security environment. In the initial environment of uncertainty, all traffic at the border was subjected to increased scrutiny, and this produced extensive border delays that, in the longer term, were inconsistent with the high level of economic integration between Canada and the U.S. While the use of National Guard troops to augment border personnel had some positive effects on border delays, it was clear that this was not a viable permanent solution. Instead, border authorities turned to a risk management approach in which the nature of the inspection reflected the level of potential risk. Unknown travellers received the highest level of scrutiny; those who furnished additional information and who had a documented record of lawful behaviour received expedited treatment at the border.

Canada and the U.S. have both relied on the risk management approach to strike a balance between security and mobility in the post 9/11 security environment. The philosophy behind this approach is stated in the following recommendation from the 9/11 Commission (2004): 'Programs to speed known travelers should be a higher priority, permitting inspectors to focus on greater risks.' This risk management strategy has been a cornerstone of bilateral and trilateral initiatives such as the December 2001 Canada–U.S. Smart Border Declaration and the March 2005 Security and Prosperity Partnership of North America. In terms of concrete programs, the risk management approach has been applied to the movement of people through the NEXUS trusted-traveller program and the FAST program for commercial shippers.

Given that the risk management approach has now been in place for some time, it is possible to analyse its results. The primary means of addressing the issue in this study is to examine changes for northbound and southbound trade flows crossing individual U.S. ports of entry. This analysis will reveal both the overall impacts of post-9/11 security procedures on trade flows, as well as any differences between ports. The potential for differential port effects exists because individual ports may have different mixes of travellers and therefore different de facto levels of security. Also, enrolment rates in programs such as FAST may differ between ports because some freight carriers and shippers may be very well informed about these programs and others less so. For example, enrolment rates are likely to be high for the automotive sector of the economy, where large firms dominate the trade flows. On the other hand, smaller exporters or carriers may be either less informed or less able to bear the costs of enrolment.

The other approach that is frequently discussed in the post-9/11 context is the use of a 'perimeter' approach to security. The primary element of this approach is the transfer of security resources from the Canada–U.S. border to the external North American border. One example of this approach can be found in the commitment the leaders of Canada, the United States, and Mexico made in the Security and Prosperity Partnership (2005a) to 'establish a common approach to security to protect North America from external threats.' A specific aspect of this general objective was the goal, stated in the Security and Prosperity Partnership (2005b), of creating a 'single, integrated global enrollment program for North American trusted traveler programs within the next 36 months' (30). This goal was met in 2006.

The creation of a perimeter security approach has been greeted with some scepticism in Canada, largely because it is associated with the type of tariff and immigration policy harmonization seen in the European Union. In the North American context, this would almost certainly involve a sacrifice of policy sovereignty by Canada. Likewise, the perimeter approach is often thought to require a Schengen-style removal of internal border controls. This would have the undesirable effect of reducing the opportunity that the Canada–U.S. border provides to limit the flow of criminal activity that originates within either North American country – a point emphasized at several times by the Canadian Senate Committee on National Security and Defence (2005).

In practice, however, many of the benefits of perimeter clearance can be provided without moving all the way to the European model. For example, the strategy outlined in the Perimeter Clearance Coalition (2002) advocated the use of joint personnel and shared databases to evaluate travellers and shipments at the point of entry to North America (defined to include just Canada and the U.S. in this coalition's document). For people, this would involve the issuance of a travel card that would identify the traveller and the (possibly different) privileges the traveller has for each country. For goods, the general approach would be to clear items away from the physical border as much as possible. In particular, items arriving from outside the Canada–U.S. perimeter would be inspected at the point of arrival and could then receive expedited processing at the Canada–U.S. border.

The results of this study will help inform border policy in several ways. The analysis of both aggregate and port-specific trade effects could provide some measure of the effectiveness of risk management techniques at the border. While we will not be able to quantify any impacts on security, we will observe the impact of the security regime on trade levels. This will provide some estimate of the pay-offs to Canada from cooperating with the United States on border security. Likewise, we will have some general indication of the return on the binational investment in risk management programs.

3 Overview of Canada–U.S. Trade in Goods

As noted in the previous chapter, the primary focus of this study is on identifying and evaluating the impact of post-9/11 security developments on bilateral trade. In this regard, it would seem that some basic information about Canada–U.S. merchandise trade would be useful background for the reader.

Aggregate Trade in Goods

Trade between the United States and Canada is the largest bilateral trading relationship in the world. While the importance of the United States as a trading partner is well known to Canadians, the importance of Canada as a trading partner is often unappreciated in the United States. Yet while increasing public and media attention in the United States is focused on that country's growing trade interdependence and trade deficits with China, Canada continues to be the single largest market for U.S. exports, as well as the largest individual country exporter to the United States.

Figure 3.1 provides a broad perspective on the relative importance of Canada as a trading partner with the United States. Specifically, it shows the share of U.S. exports that went to Canada relative to other major trading partners in 2003, as well as the share of U.S. imports originating in Canada and other regions for that same year. Exports to Canada accounted for almost 24 per cent of total U.S. merchandise exports, while imports from Canada accounted for almost 19 per cent of total U.S. merchandise imports. It is noteworthy that Canada's importance as a domestic market for U.S.-originated goods is greater than that of the Euro Area and Japan combined. Thus, while access to the U.S. market is of critical importance to Canadian-based firms, access to the Canadian market is certainly a relevant concern to U.S.-based companies.

Historical bilateral trade flows understate the importance of a smoothly functioning border between the two countries, since much of the production that takes place in each country relies on just-in-time supply of inputs shipped across the border. As Bonsor (2004, 2), among others, notes: 'Supply chains in many manufacturing sectors span the border on a daily basis. In the automobile sector, assembly plants in both countries have contracts with suppliers located across the Canada–U.S. border that specify delivery of parts in periods as short as six hours.' He goes on to note that most high-volume manufacturing operations have extended supply chains with just-in-time delivery of parts. Hence, disruptions to trade flows are damaging not just to bilateral economic integration, but also to the efficiencies of the two domestic economies.

The recent behaviour of Canada–U.S. merchandise trade flows is summarized by data reported in Table 3.1. What is clearly evident is the abrupt and substantial decrease in the nominal value of U.S. exports to and imports from Canada in 2001 that continued through 2002. It is tempting to interpret this information as prima facie evidence of the disruptive impact that 9/11 had on bilateral trade. Since a statistical evaluation of the impact of 9/11 on bilateral trade is the main focus of this study, we will refrain from giving away the 'punch line' too soon in our story; however, we will note here that other factors might be implicated in the absolute decline in bilateral trade over the 2001–2 periods. In particular, real economic growth in North America weakened substantially during that period, as suggested by the unemployment rate in the United States, which increased from 4 per cent in 2000 to 5.8 per cent in 2002. Our statistical analysis will try to hold constant the influence of factors other than border security responses to 9/11 so that the unique influence of 9/11 can be identified.

Composition of Merchandise Trade

Notwithstanding the large absolute volume of bilateral trade, the industrial composition of traded goods is fairly concentrated. By way of illustration, Table 3.2 reports the leading Canadian exports to the United States at the five-digit level of the North American Industrial

Classification System (NAICS). Specifically, Table 3.2 reports the value of U.S. imports from Canada for the fifteen largest importing industries in 2004 expressed in millions of current U.S. dollars. The fifteen industries identified account for around 55 per cent of total Canadian exports to the United States in that year. Automobiles and motor vehicles alone accounted for over 16 per cent of the value of total Canadian exports. Total exports of the five segments of the broader transportation equipment sector (NAICS 33611, 33641, 33631, 33612, and 33637) accounted for approximately 22 per cent of the value of U.S. merchandise imports from Canada. Obviously, the impact of post-9/11 border security measures on Canadian exports to the United States will be influenced strongly by the experience of the transportation equipment sector, and, in particular, by the motor vehicle sector.

The industrial composition of U.S. exports to Canada is less concentrated than the industrial composition of U.S. imports from Canada. Nevertheless, transportation equipment exports to Canada are quite important for the United States. Table 3.3 reports leading U.S. merchandise exports to Canada for 2004. Autos and motor vehicles accounted for slightly more than 9 per cent of all U.S. merchandise exports to Canada in 2004. The six transportation equipment–related sectors identified in Table 3.3 (NAICs 33611, 33639, 33631, 33635, 33641 and 33612) collectively accounted for almost 25 per cent of U.S. exports to Canada. It is clear that the transportation equipment industry is a major factor in the high degree of integrated production that characterizes the North American economy. The impact of 9/11 on bilateral trade in transportation equipment is therefore an important focus for policy makers.

While the absolute and relative importance of specific industries in overall bilateral trade flows varies somewhat over time, specific sectors have tended to dominate trade flows in terms of their overall volumes. The data reported in Tables 3.4 and 3.5 illustrate this point, as they show the percentages of total U.S. imports from Canada and total U.S. exports to Canada accounted for by the ten leading industries in 1998, along with the percentages of total imports and exports accounted for by those industries in 2004. With respect to U.S. imports from Canada (Table 3.4), the share accounted for by autos and motor vehicles decreased somewhat between 1998 and 2004. Conversely, the share of Canadian exports accounted for by oil and gas jumped substantially between those two years, reflecting perhaps in large measure an increase in energy prices in 2004. Nevertheless, transportation equipment, wood and paper products, energy, and metals are the durable leading Canadian export sectors.

In the case of U.S. exports to Canada, transportation equipment is the major industry in both 1998 and 2004, and there is, if anything, an increase in its relative importance between the two years. Various technology-intensive industries are also important sources of U.S. exports to Canada in both years, notably computer equipment, semiconductors, and measuring, medical, and control instruments, although their relative share of U.S. exports to Canada was lower in 2004 than in 1998. This last observation might possibly reflect the sharp decrease in investment in information technology capital by North American companies after 2000, particularly by telecommunications carriers. This assertion is also consistent with the sharp decrease in the relative importance of computer equipment and semiconductors in overall Canadian exports to the United States between 1998 and 2004.

An inference that might be drawn from the data on the industrial composition of bilateral trade is that a focus on a relatively small number of industries, particularly the motor vehicle industry, can shed prominent light on the impact of 9/11 on bilateral trade. Equivalently, the post-9/11 experience of a relatively small number of crossings, particularly those on the border of Michigan and Ontario, will have a disproportionate impact on Canada–U.S. trade.

Leading Ports

The concentration of bilateral trade in a relatively small number of ports is illustrated by data reported in Table 3.6. Specifically, three ports of entry on the Canada–U.S. border account for the bulk of bilateral trade.[1] Two are at the border between Michigan and Ontario (Detroit and Port Huron), and one is at the border between New York and Ontario (Buffalo–Niagara Falls). The concentration of commercial shipments at the borders between Windsor and Detroit, and Sarnia and Port Huron, is to be expected given the prominence of transportation equipment in overall bilateral trade, along with the concentration of production capacity in the transportation equipment industry in the Province of Ontario and in the State of Michigan and adjacent states. However, the concentration of trade by port is greater than the relative share of transportation equipment in total bilateral trade, as most non-auto manufactured goods in Canada originate in Ontario and Quebec and also cross into the United States at entry ports in Michigan and New York State.[2]

While the focus of this study is on bilateral merchandise trade, it is useful to note that the main points of crossing for U.S. exports and imports with Canada are also the main points for personal vehicle crossings between the two countries. Specifically, the U.S. ports at Detroit, Port Huron, and Buffalo process over 50 per cent of personal vehicle crossings from Canada.[3] An unknown share of personal vehicle crossings is related to commerce. For example, managers of multinational companies with affiliates on both sides of the border are likely to cross the border on a regular basis for meetings and related activities. Hence, to the extent that personal vehicle crossings have also been substantially and adversely affected by post-9/11 developments, trade flows may be indirectly affected. In particular, management control over interaffiliate sourcing activities may be compromised by border crossing delays and difficulties, which may lead to reduced interaffiliate trade and more sourcing by affiliates from local suppliers on both sides of the border. The observation that passenger vehicle crossings are also highly concentrated at the port level further justifies a focus on the largest border crossings in our empirical work.

Modes of Transportation

The overwhelming bulk of merchandise shipped between Canada and the United States employs surface modes of transportation, essentially truck and rail. In 2002, around 61 per cent (by value) of U.S. imports from Canada were shipped by truck and an additional 24 per cent were was shipped by rail. For U.S. exports to Canada, approximately 78 per cent were shipped by truck and 9 per cent by rail. The relative importance of energy imports from Canada accounts for the fact that pipelines are also a significant mode of transportation for Canadian exports to the United States (around 11 per cent in 2002), whereas pipelines account for only 1 per cent of U.S. exports to Canada by mode of shipment.[4] To a large extent, truck movements of imports and exports are relatively short-haul, and the goods carried are non-bulk and relatively high value. Railways concentrate on bulk commodities and goods moving relatively long distances.

Vulnerability of Trade

The preceding information regarding the composition of bilateral trade, as well as concentration by port and mode of shipment, provides potentially useful insights into the vulnerability of bilateral trade to security-related disruptions. Focusing on the composition of bilateral trade, Goldfarb and Robson (2003) evaluate and rank the sensitivity of specific Canadian exports to the United States to security-related disruptions based on five characteristics: physical security; mode of transport; time sensitivity; susceptibility to disruptions in movement of people; and ease of substitution by U.S. production.

Physical security refers to the ease with which terrorists can plant something threatening in a shipment. Electricity and other uniform commodities that travel in secure forms, such as electronic data and (to some extent) oil and natural gas in pipelines, are relatively secure. Conversely, commodities such as chemicals and food products are relatively insecure. With respect to mode of transport, Goldfarb and Robson (2003) argue that goods transported by rail are relatively simple to monitor, travel on dedicated routes, and are unlikely to sit idle in insecure locations. Consequently, goods shipped by truck are more susceptible to security-related border disruptions than goods shipped by rail.

Industries in which just-in-time delivery is important, such as auto assembly, or in which perishability is a factor, such as fresh foods, are examples of time-sensitive commodities for which shipment delays significantly degrade the economic value of the shipments. As noted above, the movement of people across borders can be a complement to the movement of goods. For example, the movement of salespeople and engineers can be strongly complementary to the cross-border sale of electronic and pharmaceutical products. Impediments to the movement of people working in such industries translate into impediments to cross-border trade in those industries. Canadian production that can be easily substituted for by U.S. production is particularly vulnerable to border delays because the additional costs incurred in shipping goods from Canada could cause buyers to source their supplies in the United States.

Robson and Goldfarb (2003) combine these different measures into an overall index of vulnerability. Automobiles and parts are among the most vulnerable sectors, given the highly integrated nature of production, which is critically dependent on time-sensitive cross-border shipments. Aerospace products, processed food products, and machinery and equipment are also relatively vulnerable sectors. In total, the authors identify around 43 per cent of total domestic goods exported from Canada to the United States as being highly vulnerable to border disruptions.

Summary

Bilateral trade between Canada and the United States is large. It is also relatively concentrated. The transportation equipment sector, in particular, is of major importance, and this sector is economically vulnerable to border disruptions. The overall impact of 9/11 on bilateral trade may therefore reflect, to a significant extent, the responses of automobile assemblers and parts suppliers on both sides of the border, as well as those of the authorities responsible for managing the operations of the major ports along the border between Ontario and Michigan and New York State. Since most goods traded between Canada and the United States are shipped by truck (and, to a much lesser extent, rail), and since a small number of ports are responsible for clearing a disproportionately large share of U.S. exports and imports with Canada, a focus on changes in trade flows at the major U.S. land ports of entry encompasses the bulk of the bilateral trade experience.

4 The Impacts of Border Security – Review of the Literature

It was quickly recognized that security-related disruptions to bilateral trade were severe in the immediate aftermath of 9/11. It is much less clear whether the significant trade-related impacts of 9/11 have persisted or whether the bilateral trade regime is essentially back to the status quo prior to 9/11. Indeed, to our knowledge, there has been virtually no published research focusing directly on the impact that 9/11 may have had on bilateral trade following the tragedy. Rather, most evaluations of 9/11 have focused on the consequences of border-related security disruptions on the operations and costs of shippers and manufacturers. The presumption underlying this focus is presumably that higher direct or indirect costs associated with shipping goods across the border will discourage bilateral trade, at the margin. While this presumption is certainly reasonable, the practical implications of increased transportation and related costs on trade flows will depend on other factors as well, including the ability of shippers and manufacturers to pass through higher prices to foreign buyers, as well as the willingness of manufacturers and shippers to absorb lower profit margins while continuing to sell to foreign buyers.

Hence, while increased costs associated with shipping goods across the border are not directly translatable into reduced bilateral trade, they are certainly a negative influence on trade, other things constant. In this regard, studies and evidence bearing on those costs as they were affected by 9/11 are certainly relevant background to our own study.

A wide range of explicit and implicit incremental costs have been associated with revised border security procedures post-9/11. One approach to identifying these costs involves estimating the changes in waiting times and the variability of waiting times post-9/11. A second approach estimates the impacts on shippers of longer and more variable waiting times at the border. A third utilizes evidence on the reactions of shippers to post-9/11 developments at the Canada–U.S. border. In particular, have shippers been willing to incur costs in order to mitigate border delays and uncertainties, and what are the magnitudes of the 'adjustment costs' that shippers have been willing to incur? A fourth provides some fragmentary empirical evidence regarding the extent to which commercial and personal automobile border crossings have changed over time. No available study, to our knowledge, has attempted to estimate the impact of post-9/11 developments on overall bilateral trade flows using the detailed and comprehensive approach employed in this study.[1]

Estimates of Waiting Times and Variability of Waiting Times

A variety of observers have stated that an important consequence of heightened border security procedures post-9/11 is increased waiting times at the border, with the additional associated costs of drivers' time, fuel, and so forth. In interviews with industry experts, we were told that in the post-9/11 period, shippers began adding wait time surcharges as well as fuel surcharges.[2] We were also told that increased variability of wait times at the border post-9/11 were even more troublesome for shippers than increased average wait times, since variability in wait times makes costs relatively unpredictable.[3] Information on changes in average wait times, as well as on variability of wait times, therefore provides some insight into the impacts of post-9/11 border security procedures on the costs of bilateral trade.

Unfortunately, there are no consistent data on average waiting times and variability of waiting times for the pre- and post-9/11 periods. Hence, it is not possible to report waiting time behaviour for commercial shippers on a reliable and continuous basis over a time period that includes the pre- and post-9/11 experience. What *are* available are individual surveys at different points in time that provide 'snapshots' of waiting time experiences of shippers.

Pre-9/11

It is certainly true that positive waiting times and variability of waiting times existed prior to 9/11. For example, a survey undertaken for the

U.S. Federal Highway Administration (FHA) examined hours of delay for commercial motor vehicles passing through selected U.S. border crossings with Canada and Mexico in 2001. The waiting times at the four northern border crossings in the study (Ambassador Bridge, Blaine, Blue Water Bridge, and Peace Bridge) are of particular interest and are reported in Table 4.1. Three wait time estimates are provided: (1) baseline time, which is the time needed to travel through the port of entry at low-volume conditions; (2) average time needed to travel through the port of entry; and (3) 95th percentile time, which is the time within which 95 per cent of the trucks surveyed travelled the relevant distance.

In this FHA survey, actual travel times start from the first queuing point before the border and end when the vehicle is released from inspection. Not included are the congestion delays that occur prior to the queuing for the crossing. The latter delays can be significant when traffic must move through heavily built up streets in cities such as Windsor, Ontario, and Blaine, Washington.

Several inferences can be drawn from Table 4.1. One is that crossing times were generally longer entering the U.S. than entering Canada. A second is that there was substantial variability in wait times. This is shown by the reported differences between baseline wait time and the average wait time, as well as the difference between the average wait time and the 95th percentile time. These differences are especially marked for inbound traffic to the United States at the Port Huron (Blue Water) and Buffalo (Peace Bridge) crossings. The range in wait times is larger for traffic inbound to the United States than for traffic inbound to Canada. The survey concluded that there was a definite relationship between the number of booths open and the travel time through the crossing. Decisions on how many booths to open at any given time are apparently not made purely with mobility or crossing times in mind.

Bonsor (2004, 9) agrees that border delays existed before the events of 9/11, with the root cause being that physical infrastructure at most major border crossings could not handle the large increase in truck traffic that had occurred over the previous fifteen years. As well, border crossing staffing levels were inadequate in a number of cases. Between 1987 and 2000, cross-border commercial truck traffic grew by 92 per cent, from around 19,000 crossings per day to around 37,000 a day. Neither the infrastructure nor the system for clearing traffic kept up with this growth.

Post-9/11

One early survey of Canadian carriers reported a 20 per cent increase in border delays going southbound and a 12 per cent increase in delays going northbound shortly after 9/11.[4] The survey was reported in August 2002, and the findings are likely to be sensitive to the timing of the survey. In particular, the border delays might have been much worse in the immediate post-9/11 period had it not been for the added presence of the U.S. National Guard at the border. The removal of these extra agents from the border in July 2002 could be expected to increase border delays, and Goldfarb and Robson (2003) report that delays did, indeed, become more frequent and more variable in terms of crossing time required once the National Guard was removed.

Somewhat more recent estimates of wait times and variability of wait times are provided by the Canada Customs and Revenue Agency. Wait times for commercial vehicles at the four busiest northern border crossings apparently fell in late 2001 and early 2002 but rose again in early 2002, after which there was no obvious trend through March 2003, although there were large intervening fluctuations in average monthly wait times. Average wait time for inbound traffic to the United States in March 2003 was estimated at 15 to 16 minutes, which is actually below the estimate of average wait times for inbound commercial traffic reported in Table 4.1. This survey also reports substantial variability around the estimated average wait time. Specifically, the estimated standard deviation of average daily wait time increased from around 5 minutes to around 15 minutes in the first half of 2002. Subsequently, there was no obvious continued trend increase in variability, although the estimated standard deviation of wait times increased to between 20 and 25 minutes in December 2002 before declining to around 18 minutes in March 2003.

Lee and her colleagues (2005) report the results of a survey of delays at the border for surface shipments originating in Quebec. Using data from the U.S. Department of Homeland Security (DHS), an average of delays at the border during the two p.m. rush hour was calculated for every Wednesday in the month of May for the years 2003, 2004, and 2005. The average time waiting by Quebec truckers to reach the border was around 32 minutes.

In the absence of a comprehensive time series detailing average wait times and the variability of wait times around the average, it is impossible to be conclusive regarding whether border congestion problems have been ameliorated in recent years. Certainly, they have not been eliminated, as indicated by border wait times reported by the DHS for 12 December 2005. Table 4.2 reports the average wait times reported for a number of U.S. crossing points for commercial vehicles entering the United States at the local times shown. There are substantial differences from location to location, with some crossings reporting minimal delays and others reporting very substantial delays. For example, the reported wait time for commercial vehicles at Emerson/Pembina was over 90 minutes, while it was 45 minutes at the important Sarnia/Port Huron crossing. It is relevant to note that there were no significant delays reported by those using expedited facilities, most notably the FAST program. Hence, while there was a 45-minute delay for commercial traffic using the non-expedited lanes at the Sarnia/Port Huron crossing, there was no reported wait for commercial traffic using the expedited inspection process at that crossing. This observation suggests that a substantial number of commercial shippers find it too costly or difficult to join the FAST program, notwithstanding the associated savings in time they would enjoy at border crossings. We will consider this issue further in our concluding chapter.[5]

In addition to the time spent waiting to reach the border, shippers must spend additional time being cleared through the border. In a 2005 report, the Coalition for Secure and Trade-Efficient Borders reported that since the Smart Border Declaration of 2001, estimated processing times for shipments entering the United States from Canada increased 300 per cent, from 45 seconds to more than 135 seconds per truck at the end of 2004. The increased processing time is a consequence of a 'layering' of security requirements for North American businesses pursuant to 9/11. The inference that might be drawn is that wait times have increased post-9/11.[6]

Estimated Cost and Profitability Impacts

Border congestion and associated delays can be expected to increase costs.[7] Taylor, Robideaux, and Jackson (2003) provide a catalogue of relevant costs. Specifically, they identify two broad categories of costs for manufacturers shipping goods across the border. One category is related to increased transit times and greater uncertainty about transit times. The second includes more general border-related costs, including administrative costs associated with complying with customs procedures. As such, the border cost estimates they supply are arguably broader than those which are strictly associated with security procedures pursuant to 9/11. Nevertheless, a major set of costs arise as a result of backups at primary border inspection sites, as well as increased time spent at secondary inspection sites.

Uncertainty associated with expected transit time results in costs associated with the inefficient operation of shipping and manufacturing capacities, as well as higher inventory levels. The authors generate cost estimates based on information gathered during the summer of 2002 through interviews with shippers and other industry participants, as well as site visits. They estimate that border-related costs range from US$7.52 billion to $13.20 billion, with a 'most likely' cost estimate of $10.3 billion. The bulk of these costs are associated with the first category of cost drivers, that is, increased waiting and increased uncertainty of waiting.[8] The authors note that the estimate of $10.3 billion represents 2.7 per cent of bilateral merchandise trade in 2001. The authors do not provide any estimates of the impact of these additional costs on trade flows. Moreover, they do not estimate cost impacts on tourism, or the impact of those costs on tourism-related trade.

In a similar study, Bonsor (2004) argues that significant delays at major border crossings have pushed transportation costs above an efficient level. His study estimates that for most transportation carriers an hour's delay costs between $45 and $55, although he acknowledges that this is a crude estimate. Belzer (2004) looks at the costs of delay at the Ambassador Bridge to the 'average' trucking company. The 'upper bounds' of added delay is estimated to add between $24.4 billion and $32.4 billion to total operating costs by the year 2030. The study predicts that by the year 2010, the annual cost of border delays budgeted by freight shippers will be $1.9 billion to $2.5 billion.

DAMF Consulting (2005) provides a relatively recent estimate of the cost impacts of U.S. border security measures on Canadian carriers. These costs include the consequences of longer border crossing times, as well as the transaction costs associated with meeting the 'paperwork' burden imposed by new security procedures. It estimates that 60 to 90 minutes have been added to the average transit time for truck movements crossing the Canada–U.S. border and that the estimated annual cost impact of security measures on the Canadian trucking industry is between $179 million and $406 million in 2005 dollars. This number represents approximately 4 per cent of the total expenses of Canadian for-hire transborder carriers.

Partial or Indirect Estimates of Impacts of Post-9/11 Developments on Border Crossings

An alternative approach to measuring the impact of border delays is to focus on reductions in border crossings. Globerman (2005) relates the number of crossings of commercial vehicles (trucks) into the United States from Canada to the real GDP of the United States. Observers argue that while congestion occurs on both sides of the border, more often it is produced on the U.S. side (i.e., by traffic entering the U.S.).[9] Hence, to the extent that trade flows are being curtailed by increased congestion at the border, one would expect to observe it most readily in terms of Canadian shipments to the United States. In relating Canadian truck crossings solely to U.S. real GDP, Globerman is obviously ignoring other potential determinants of Canadian export activity – a point to which we return in a later chapter. Nevertheless, changes in real economic activity are certainly an important determinant of trade activity by themselves.

Choosing 1994 as a base year, Globerman creates index values for both truck crossings and real U.S. GDP for the years 1995–2002. The index series for truck crossings reaches a peak in the year 2000, declines in 2001, and then increases in 2002. Real GDP increases consistently from 1995 to 2000, levels off in 2001, and then increases in 2002. A ratio of the index of truck crossings to the index of real GDP increases from 1996 to 1999 and then declines slightly in 2000. There is a more substantial decline in the ratio in 2001, with no change in 2002. The lower values of the ratio in 2001 and 2002 compared to 2000 are certainly consistent with a post-9/11 impact on trade flows; however, the fact that the decline apparently commenced in 2000 is inconsistent with a unique 9/11 impact.

Globerman also relates the nominal value of Canadian exports to the nominal value of U.S. GDP. The ratio of nominal Canadian exports (converted to USD) to nominal U.S. GDP increases consistently and strongly from 1997 to 2000 and then declines sharply in 2001. A further and more modest decline is observed for 2002. To the extent that border crossing times for trucks were increasing even prior to 9/11, it is reasonable to expect that efforts would be made to utilize trucking capacity more efficiently in order to economize on border crossings. For example, larger trucks might be used, with the capacity of the trucks more fully utilized. If this were true, simply counting truck crossings could result in biased estimates of the impact of border congestion on the actual value of merchandise crossing the border. Specifically, it would tend to overstate the impact. This realistic possibility underscores the relevance of examining trade flows.

In this regard, Globerman's estimate of trade flows relative to GDP shows a similar pattern over time to his estimate of truck crossings relative to GDP. Both estimates of the trade-related impacts of border congestion suggest that there was a substantial disruption of Canadian exports to the U.S. in 2001, which is entirely believable given that the border essentially closed in the immediate aftermath of 9/11 for about one week and that there were substantial delays in the aftermath of the border reopening. His estimates are more equivocal regarding whether the impacts of border congestion on trade persisted beyond 2001, although they appear to have done so.[10]

Globerman also reports a simple test of the impact of post-9/11 border security procedures on personal vehicle crossings from Canada into the United States. Personal vehicle crossings might reflect both tourism-related travel and business-related travel, and available information does not permit separate identification of the two. In the case of tourism from Canada to the United States, a relevant 'control' variable would seem to be the Canada–U.S. exchange rate. Specifically, a higher (lower) value of the Canadian dollar should encourage (discourage) tourism from Canada to the United States. Obviously, other factors influence tourism traffic. Hence, Globerman's analysis is, at best, suggestive. He presents data showing that a substantial depreciation in the Canadian dollar took place between 1997 and 1998 that was mirrored by a substantial decline in an index of personal vehicle crossings from Canada to the United States. The exchange rate was relatively unchanged from 1998 to 2000, as was the index of personal vehicle crossings. There was a sharp decrease in the exchange rate between 2000 and 2001, again mirrored by a substantial decrease in the index of vehicle crossings. This same pattern was repeated for the period 2001–2 – that is, both the exchange rate and the index of vehicle crossings declined; however, the relative decrease in vehicle crossings given the exchange rate decrease from 2001 to 2002 was substantially greater than the relationship between the two series for earlier periods. That is, the index of vehicle crossings declined in 2002 by a greater amount than one would have anticipated based on the experience of earlier periods.

Other Evidence

Goldfarb and Robson (2003) also look at Canadian exports to the United States in the immediate aftermath of 9/11. They effectively create a cross-section of data by classifying industries into those more or less likely to be adversely affected by border disruptions, using select characteristics of the industries that were discussed earlier. They then examine the behaviour of Canadian merchandise exports to the U.S. over the period August 2000–October 2001. They find that exports for industries rated as more vulnerable to border disruptions declined more than they did for exports as a whole, which provides consistent support for other studies that found substantial curtailment of shipments from Canada to the United States in the aftermath of the 9/11 attack.

Goldfarb and Robson try to get a sense of the expected longer-run disruptions to bilateral trade by comparing the behaviour of the share prices of publicly traded companies in 'border-dependent' industries with share prices of companies in less border-dependent industries. They also compare Canadian and U.S. stock price indexes on the basis that Canadian shares are more likely to capture vulnerability to border disruptions than U.S. share prices, given the proportionally greater importance of border-related trade to the Canadian economy. With respect to the first point of focus, they found that the share prices of companies in the most trade-sensitive sectors did not fall dramatically more than the overall index, which was itself sent lower by declining share prices among financial services companies, department stores, and hospitality industries in the wake of the 9/11 attack.[11] With respect to the second point of focus, the authors compared the performance of the S&P 500 index to that of the TSE 300. Relative to 10 September 2001, the TSE 300 fell by more than the S&P composite for most months following the 9/11 attack, although the difference in the relative sizes of the declines in the two indices was small. The stock market evidence reported by Goldfarb and Robson is therefore consistent with an interpretation that substantial border security–related disruptions to trade were fairly short-run in nature.[12]

MacPherson and McConnell (2005) report the results of a mail survey that was distributed during the late summer of 2004 to executives of business establishments located in southern Ontario and western New York State. The survey focused on the differences between the pre- and post-9/11 border crossing experiences of the respondents. Regarding imports, more than half the Canadian respondents identified negative impacts of 9/11, while some 38 per cent of American respondents indicated negative impacts. More than three-quarters of the Ontario executives identified negative impacts of 9/11 on their exporting activities, while less than one-quarter of American executives reported such effects. The most important impact cited in the survey was the increases in costs associated with 'transit time and abnormal border delays.' Unfortunately, the survey provides no information as a basis for quantitative estimates of any reductions in bilateral trade flows.

To the extent that enhanced border security procedures have added significant additional costs to cross-border shipping, one might expect companies involved in cross-border exporting and importing to take advantage of programs and initiatives that expedite commercial cross-border shipping, even if those programs and initiatives have costs of their own. A significant response on the part of companies to border-related delays and uncertainties would be indirect evidence of the significance of the costs associated with delays and uncertainties.

In MacPherson and McConnell's survey, about one-third of Canadian respondents reported that they were planning to reduce their dependence on the United States and other foreign sources of materials and components. Slightly more than one-quarter were planning to select alternative Canada–U.S. border crossings, while around 20 per cent were planning alternative transport routes to the border. None of the Canadian respondents indicated that they were considering moving production in the United States back to Canada. Less than half the U.S. respondents reported any intention to take action in response to transit times and abnormal border delays. Of those indicating such intentions, about 40 per cent reported plans to reduce dependence on Canada and other foreign sources of materials and components. Approximately 20 per cent planned to select alternative Canada–U.S. border crossings. About 28 per cent of Canadian respondents and 14 per cent of U.S. respondents indicated the possibility that increased security regulations would lead them to substitute higher-cost North American products for lower-cost offshore products. This latter response suggests that border security costs may be proportionately higher for container cargo carried by ship compared to truck transport.

Globerman (2005) also investigated potential changes in shipment mode or shipment patterns in the post-9/11 period. It was noted earlier that trucks pose a greater security threat than trains. One might therefore expect that shippers using trucks would face relatively higher costs from border security procedures than those using rail.[13] If these added costs were substantial, one would expect them to encourage some substitution away from truck shipments towards rail shipments. To evaluate this, Globerman calculated Canadian merchandise exports to the United States carried by truck relative to shipments carried by rail over the period 1994 to 2003. Over the period 1994 to 2000, the ratio equals 2.57. It equals 2.46 for 2001–3. This difference is not statistically significant, which suggests that there was no meaningful substitution away from trucking towards rail on the part of Canadian exporters.

Globerman also investigated whether shippers had altered their ports of entry to reduce waiting times. Obviously, shippers could not be expected to take major detours from their pre-9/11 routes in response to the waiting times identified earlier; however, some switching between ports that are relatively closely located might be anticipated if the border-related disruptions were severe and varied by port. In particular, the Port Huron port of entry was characterized by higher average waiting times and greater variability in waiting times compared to Detroit in the early post-9/11 period. However, Globerman found that the shares of Canadian exports crossing through the Port Huron and Detroit ports were virtually the same for the period 2002–3 as they were for the period 1994–2000.[14]

Finally, Lee and her colleagues (2005) attempt to estimate the impact of delayed border crossings on Quebec exports to the United States by imputation. Specifically, they employ an estimated average time for surface shipments to cross the border from Quebec and multiply that by an estimated cost to truckers associated with that average time delay. The product term is effectively an estimate of the cost per individual truck crossing associated with waiting to clear U.S. customs. They then multiply the product term by the annual number of truck crossings for shipments originating from Quebec. This results in an estimated total cost of security-specific border delays to Quebec shippers of around C$70 million in 2004. The impact on exports from Quebec to the United States is imputed by assuming that all of the security-specific costs are passed on to U.S. buyers. The resulting decrease in exports will then be the product term of the price elasticity of U.S. demand for Quebec exports (assumed to be –0.8) and the $70 million estimated cost, or a reduction in Quebec exports of $56 million in 2004. By way of comparison, Quebec's merchandise exports to the United States in 2004 were around $56 billion. Hence, the estimated trade impact is relatively small.

Summary

A review of a variety of different sources of evidence on the impact of post-9/11 border-related disruptions suggests that significant additional costs and delays were imposed on shippers in the immediate aftermath of 9/11. Efforts made by the two national governments to mitigate the impacts of the disruptions – in particular, the dispatching of the National Guard to border crossings – did apparently mitigate some of the adverse impacts and facilitated reductions in delay times; however, it appears that delays and timing uncertainties associated with border crossings remain greater problems than they were prior to 9/11.

Given the apparently non-trivial magnitude of the costs to shippers associated with border crossing delays, it would be surprising if there had been no impact on bilateral trade in the post-9/11 period. Nevertheless, there is very little direct evidence available on this issue, and the limited evidence available that directly or indirectly relates to this issue is inconclusive at best. In the next section of this study, we outline our empirical approach to identifying the extent to which bilateral trade has been affected by post-9/11 border disruptions, as well as whether the effects are concentrated in specific industrial sectors or geographic regions.

5 Study Methodology

In this chapter we discuss conceptual and pedagogical issues surrounding the specification and estimation of a model of bilateral trade between Canada and the United States. We have chosen to identify the impacts of 9/11 on bilateral trade through an estimated model of bilateral trade spanning a time period before and after the 9/11 attack. Specifically, we specify and estimate separate equations for goods crossing the border from the United States to Canada and from Canada to the United States over the period extending from the first quarter of 1996 or 1997 through the second quarter of 2005.[1] The estimation is undertaken both for pooled samples representing all U.S. merchandise exports and imports crossing the land border with Canada over that period, as well as for exports and imports crossing the U.S. border at specific land ports.

The Gravity Model

Standard statistical models of international trade share a common framework known as the gravity equation.[2] In the 'bare-bones' gravity equation, trade between a pair of countries is modelled as an increasing function of their sizes and a decreasing function of the physical distance between the two countries. All other things constant, the larger the size of a country, the greater the demand of its residents for all types of goods, including goods produced in other countries. Hence, trade between any two countries should increase as the size of each trading partner increases. Physical distance is an indirect measure of the transportation costs associated with international trade. The greater the physical distance between any two countries, the greater should be the transportation costs holding constant the mix of goods traded and the mode of shipment.

Models of international trade recognize that this bare-bones gravity model must be augmented by other variables in order to more fully explain the determinants of international trade. An additional variable frequently included in trade equations is per capita income. It has been observed that richer countries engage more intensively in international trade than do poorer countries. An explanation offered is that a 'taste for variety' increases as consumers become wealthier. Since imports often are differentiated from domestically produced goods, wealthier consumers are more likely to demand imported products than are poorer consumers. Hence, trade equations often include the per capita income levels of the trading partners to capture this taste-for-variety influence. A second additional variable is a measure of legal trade barriers between the trading partners. For example, trade models frequently include a variable identifying whether or not the trading partners are members of a free trade area or a common market (Frankel and Rose 2002; deGroot et al. 2004). All other things constant, bilateral trade should be greater between countries that are members of a preferential trading arrangement, since tariffs and possibly non-tariff barriers will be reduced by such arrangements.

An additional set of variables that is often suggested to influence trade volumes includes characteristics that can be related to transaction costs associated with international trade, particularly the costs of identifying trading opportunities, making the appropriate commercial contacts, and so forth. The characteristics that have been identified in a number of studies represent cultural and institutional differences between countries that are suggested to increase such transaction costs. An example is whether or not countries share a common language. A common language should make it easier and cheaper to negotiate transactions, among other things. Another example is whether or not countries have similar legal and regulatory environments. Such similarities should reduce costs associated with a range of activities from writing contracts to meeting packaging requirements for products. Some studies also include the 'stocks' of immigrants from one country that are residents of the second country (Gould 1994; Rauch 2001; Combes, Lafourcade, and Mayer 2003). The notion here is that immigrants can function effectively as knowledgeable agents, which can help mitigate transaction costs associated with social and cultural differences between countries.

Several other variables have been included in studies of international trade. Exchange rates are a potentially important determinant of trade flows. Hence, in some studies, variables are included that identify whether or not the trading partners share a common currency or whether one of the national currencies is linked to the other through a fixed exchange rate. A number of economists have argued that a common currency boosts trade and direct investment between countries (Courchene and Harris 1999). Evidence on the substantial magnitude of this trade-boosting effect is provided by Frankel and Rose (2002), although the result reported by Frankel and Rose has been questioned by others. The analogue is that an unstable currency arrangement will discourage trade and direct investment, other things constant.

Changes in exchange rates may alter overall patterns of trade to the extent that they do not simply reflect relative changes in domestic costs. For example, the depreciation of Canada's nominal exchange rate in the 1990s was not mirrored by increases in Canadian domestic prices relative to U.S. domestic prices. This meant that the Canadian exchange rate depreciated in both real and nominal terms. A consequence was a surge in Canadian exports to the U.S. relative to Canadian imports from the U.S. (Globerman and Storer 2005). Hence, in an equation seeking to identify the determinants of trade flows from one country to another, the bilateral exchange rate relationship is a candidate for inclusion as an independent variable.

The traditional gravity model specification can therefore be summarized as shown in the equation below. Since a number of the independent variables influence the dependent variable in a multiplicative form – for example, the product term of the GDPs of the trading partners – those variables are converted to (natural) log values so that the equation can be estimated through linear regression techniques.

$$\ln (T_{ij}) = B_0 + B_1\ln (GDP_i) + B_2\ln (GDP_j) + B_3\ln (gdp_i) + B_4\ln (gdp_j) + B_kZ_k \ldots\ldots + B_lZ_l + e_{ij}$$

In the equation, the dependent variable is measured as the natural logarithm of the volume of merchandise going from country i to country j. The 'GDP' variables measure the total GDP of countries i and j, respectively, while the 'gdp' variables represent the per capita income levels of each country. Other variables that might be included in the gravity equation, depending on the identities of the sample countries and whether one is measuring a gravity equation across countries for a given period of time (cross-section) or for a given set of countries over time (time series), are captured in the Z terms. The e term represents the residuals or estimation error term.

Application of the Gravity Equation to the Study

As noted above, we are specifically interested in whether and how trade flows between Canada and the United States were affected by border disruptions and ensuing government efforts to mitigate the disruptions in the post-9/11 period. Hence, we are interested in estimating a gravity model in the bilateral context over time. One consequence is that a number of variables that are typically included in cross-section models of trade will not be relevant to our study, since they do not vary over time. For example, physical border distances between exporters and importers will be constant for any given distribution of products.[3] The commonality of English language use encompassing most bilateral traders will also be constant. The legal and regulatory institutions of the two countries have changed modestly over the past few decades, but the changes have tended to be similar in the two countries.[4] Changes in social and cultural institutions have also arguably changed only modestly over the past two decades or so. In any case, the long and extensive history of trade, direct investment, tourism, and migration between the United States and Canada arguably obviates the practical importance of transaction cost considerations related to differences in social and cultural institutions. Since we are interested in the determinants of changing bilateral trade over a relatively short period of time, we can ignore the influence of both time-invariant factors and factors that have changed relatively slowly over time.[5]

A number of time-sensitive variables are, however, potentially relevant determinants of bilateral trade flows in our sample. They include the GDP values and per capita income values for the United States and Canada. Since we measure trade flows in nominal (U.S.) dollar values, we should measure GDP and per capita income values in nominal U.S. dollars as well – for example, current Canadian dollar values translated into U.S. dollars at the current exchange rate. The behaviour of the Canada–U.S. exchange rate over the sample period is also potentially relevant. The Canadian dollar depreciated in value against the U.S. dollar over much of the sample period of our study, and all other things constant, this depreciation should have encouraged an increase in Canadian exports to the U.S. and a decrease in U.S. exports to Canada.

The time-sensitive variable of most direct relevance to this study is the magnitude of the explicit and implicit costs associated with security-related disruptions at border crossings subsequent to 9/11. Conceptually, this variable would measure all of the additional costs associated with shipping goods across the Canada–U.S. border that arise exclusively from security-related regulations and inspection procedures at the border. Ideally, measures of this variable would be available on a continual basis for periods both before and after 9/11. As discussed in the preceding chapter, no such estimates are available on a time series basis. Nor, to our knowledge, is there a readily available time series estimate of waiting times and variability of waiting times that might serve as a rough proxy measure of the costs associated with complying with new security requirements, including new inspection procedures at the border.

In this context, a pragmatic approach to identifying the linkage between post-9/11 security-related changes in shipping conditions and bilateral trade is to incorporate a 'time period' variable into the model. For example, a very basic time-period model would simply use a single binary 0/1 variable to distinguish between the period prior to 9/11 and the period after 9/11.[6] This specification would allow for bilateral trade flows to be unchanged, lower, or higher after 9/11, holding other determinants of trade constant. An important presumption of this simple binary time variable specification is that the effect of 9/11 on bilateral trade is constant throughout the post-9/11 period. That is, whatever the impact of 9/11 was on trade, its magnitude is the same in every period of time subsequent to 9/11. This 'constant impact' specification is intuitively unappealing, as discussed below.

A second presumption is that the influence of the time period variable reflects the impact of security-related initiatives and not other factors that are not being held explicitly constant in the statistical model. Indeed, this presumption underlies any estimation technique where the researcher uses measures of time as proxies for unobservable events or developments. When adopting the expedient of using time as an explanatory variable in a model, the researcher invites the potential criticism that the time variable is measuring something other than what the researcher intended, or that the time variable implicitly captures the influence of factors in addition to the phenomenon of interest. In either case, it would be misleading to associate the measured impact of the time period variable on the dependent variable, in our case bilateral trade flows, exclusively with the phenomenon of interest, in our case border security–related initiatives. Hence, the burden on the researcher is to ensure that the time period specification chosen is not accidentally capturing other possible influences on the dependent variable other than the phenomenon meant to be implicitly measured by the time variable.

As suggested above, the use of a single binary time variable as a proxy for border security–related impacts on trade is intuitively unappealing. In particular, the time pattern for border security–related disruptions is likely to be more complex than that described by a simple dichotomous specification such as pre- and post-9/11. For example, the relevant literature reviewed earlier suggests that the impacts in the immediate post-9/11 period were most severe, but then were alleviated by the U.S. government making additional resources available on an emergency basis; however, after these resources were withdrawn, waiting times and waiting time variability may have increased again, albeit not to the same levels as in the immediate aftermath of 9/11. This more complex timing pattern is not captured by the binary specification for the time variable.

Another approach is to specify hypothetical time patterns whereby the linkage between the dependent variable and time is more continuous than the relationship specified by the single dichotomous time variable. For example, if one believed that adverse impacts on trade continually increased in the post-9/11 period, one might specify the time variable to take a value of zero in the pre-9/11 period and then take increasing linear or non-linear values as one moves further away in time from 9/11. If one believed that the adverse impacts on trade continually decreased after the immediate aftermath of 9/11, one might specify the time variable to take some positive value in the immediate post-9/11 period and then take consistently smaller values as one moved further away in time from 9/11.

Clearly, there are numerous possible specifications of the time variable in the absence of strong a priori expectations. Unless one has strong priors about the time pattern of security-related border disruptions, it seems advisable to use a general specification of the relationship between the dependent variable and time. To the extent that the results are plausible in light of known facts, one can be somewhat confident of having identified the true relationship between the dependent variable and time, holding other factors constant.

The most general specification would identify each sample period as having a 'unique' impact on bilateral trade, given the other independent variables. This specification would be realized by identifying a separate time variable for each time period. For example, Y_1 would take a value of 1 in the immediate post-9/11 period and zero otherwise; Y_2 would take a value of 1 in the 'next' period and zero otherwise; Y_3 would take a value of 1 in the 'third' period and zero otherwise. And so forth. This general specification allows the impact of time on the dependent variable to vary virtually continuously over time. While the approach is essentially an agnostic one, it seems more appropriate than 'forcing' specific time patterns on the data in the absence of strong theoretical reasons for one or another specific pattern.

Another concern noted earlier is the possibility that other factors influence trade flows and are not explicitly included in our model. Indeed, if the timing of these factors corresponds to the specification of our time variable, which, in turn is meant to identify border-related security disruptions, the model might mistakenly attribute changes in bilateral trade flows to border related disruptions rather than to the true determinants. A number of possibilities arise in the context of bilateral trade in the post-9/11 period. For example, changing economic and policy conditions surrounding the softwood lumber industry might have a substantial impact on Canadian lumber exports to the United States. Given the overall importance of lumber exports in total Canadian exports, one might observe a significant change in overall Canadian exports as a result. If the impact of the softwood lumber dispute was particularly strong in the post-9/11 period, the model might ascribe observed changes in Canadian trade flows to post-9/11 changes in border security procedures, rather than to changes in conditions surrounding the softwood lumber industry. As another example, changes in business cycle conditions might be particularly significant for the auto industry in the post-9/11 period. Given the importance of this industry in overall bilateral trade, a failure to explicitly identify business conditions surrounding the auto industry might lead to inadvertent statistical biases. Of particular concern is the possibility that the timing of business cycle changes for the auto industry coincide with the specification of the time period dummy variables.

Other unspecified factors may influence trade flows across virtually all commodity categories. An example is increased road congestion leading to and away from border crossings. Increased road congestion can be expected to discourage bilateral trade flows, holding other determinants constant. If access roads to border crossings became more congested simply because of a growing number of vehicles on the roads over time, bilateral trade may decrease even if border security procedures have completely benign effects. Another example is higher fuel prices, which can be expected to discourage truck shipments, including cross-border shipments.[7] To the extent that fuel prices increased in the post-9/11 period, one might ascribe reduced bilateral trade to border security procedures while ignoring the influence of higher fuel prices.

To some extent, the potential relevance of such unspecified factors can be evaluated in the context of our statistical results. For example, if U.S. imports from Canada seemed to have declined in the post-9/11 period whereas U.S. exports to Canada did not, the bilateral trade pattern would be inconsistent with the hypothesis that broad factors such as higher fuel prices had discouraged bilateral trade, since if this hypothesis were true, exports from both countries should have been affected. As another example, if bilateral trade showed a variable pattern of increasing and decreasing over the sample period, this observation would be inconsistent with the hypothesis that increased road congestion was the main factor influencing bilateral trade flows post-9/11, since traffic congestion is more likely to have increased in a monotonic fashion over time.

Specifying the Trade Equations

Ferley (2004) reports results of a parsimonious trade equation for Canadian exports and imports. Specifically, Canadian exports are specified as a function of U.S. final domestic demand and the Canada–U.S. exchange rate. He estimates an overall export growth equation, as well as separate equations for major export groups. The model for overall export growth performs better statistically than the models for individual export groups in terms of having a higher overall R-squared statistic. This latter result is not surprising, since individual product groups are more likely to be characterized by 'unique' determinants of trade such as the imposition or removal of antidumping duties or growth in demand that is unrelated to the expansion of the overall economy of the importing country. In an equation for overall exports, such idiosyncrasies are more likely to 'average out,' thereby allowing the generic explanatory variables – U.S. domestic demand and the exchange rate – to play a larger and more precise role in determining exports over time. In fact, our commodity classification is more disaggregated than Ferley's, and the influence of factors affecting trade specific to particular industries can therefore be expected to be substantial.

Ferley finds that U.S. final domestic demand growth boosts Canada's export growth, and that depreciation in the value of the Canadian dollar also boosts export growth. The impact of the exchange rate on export growth occurs with a lag that varies across major industry groups. In some cases, the lag is as long as four to eight quarters. For some groups, no significant lag can be identified. On the other hand, the impact of U.S. domestic demand on export growth was contemporaneous in virtually all cases.

Ferley also estimates equations for Canadian imports using the same basic specification as the export equation. Specifically, the import equation includes Canadian final domestic demand and the bilateral exchange rate as independent variables. These two independent variables have the expected signs. In the overall import equation, the best results were obtained when the exchange rate was averaged over a four-quarter lagged time period. The impact of the Canadian final domestic demand variable was contemporaneous.

Theoretical considerations outlined earlier in this section, along with Ferley's results, support the use of a parsimonious specification of export and import equations that include, as basic variables, a measure of final demand in the importing country and the bilateral exchange rate. Ferley's results highlight the importance of the level of industry aggregation to the statistical results obtained. As a rule, more highly aggregated industrial classifications should produce better overall statistical results than more disaggregated classifications; however, part of our interest is to identify whether border disruptions post-9/11 differed in their impacts by port. Given the concentration of commodity shipments in specific ports (e.g., autos and motor vehicle parts crossing the border between Windsor and Detroit), estimation of export and import equations at the port level is somewhat equivalent to estimation of export and import equations at the commodity level.[8] Nevertheless, in a later chapter, we try to identify whether post-9/11 security developments have differentially affected bilateral trade in major commodity categories across major ports.

Our initial focus is on overall U.S. imports from and exports to

Canada passing through all ports of entry in the United States. More precisely, our initial focus is to estimate export and import equations for U.S. trade with Canada on a pooled time-series, cross-section basis, where dummies for the ten largest ports are included as independent variables. This specification can therefore be seen as identifying the 'average' impact of other included independent variables on bilateral trade flows across all ports involved in Canada–U.S. trade.

Our initial sample time period is defined as 1996 (quarter 1) through 2001 (quarter 2) for U.S. imports and 1997 (quarter 1) through 2001 (quarter 2) for U.S. exports.[9] In choosing this initial focus, our goal was to evaluate whether a statistically reliable and relatively simple trade equation could be identified for the period prior to 9/11.[10] After identifying a reliable and relatively simple trade equation fit to trade data for the pre-9/11 period, the equation is then used to evaluate whether and how the trade regime changed in the post-9/11 period. This evaluation is performed for overall exports and imports, as well as for exports and imports for each of the ten largest U.S. ports of entry.

Data Sources

The source of data for the trade flows (T_i) is the Foreign Trade Division of the U.S. Bureau of the Census. Specifically, we purchased downloads of the bureau's unpublished database, which identifies exports and imports for every U.S. port of entry with commodity details provided at the five-digit SITC level. This database is the only source of data that reports U.S. exports and imports by individual commodity for each individual port. These data are available at a higher level of aggregation in the Transborder Surface Freight Database (TSFD) on the website of the U.S. Bureau of Transportation Statistics (BTS). For example, the TSFD provides information by port of entry aggregated over all commodities. The TSFD also provides commodity breakdowns but only at the state rather than the port level. The value-added of the foreign trade data acquired for this study is that we are able to examine changes in aggregate port-level shipments, as well as differences in commodity mixes both over time and between ports.

The surface trade data used in this study are part of the official U.S. international trade statistics. Exports from Canada to the United States are measured based on information filed with U.S. Customs, and the majority of this information is now submitted electronically. In some cases the information is filed at an inland port removed from the actual border crossing point, and there is no way to identify the actual port of entry for these shipments. Data for U.S. exports to Canada are provided to the United States by Statistics Canada under the terms of a Canada–U.S. data-sharing agreement.

While these data provide the best available figures on freight flows at the U.S. land border ports, there are several minor shortcomings. First, data for transshipments (goods passing through the United States on their way from one third country to another) are not available and so are not included in this study. Next, in order to focus on Canada–U.S. trade and to preserve comparability with the BTS data, we only include U.S. imports that originated in Canada and U.S. exports that terminated in Canada. Finally, we do not have access to a breakdown between modes of transport for the commodity/port trade flows and can only examine changes in mode by supplementing our analysis with BTS all-commodity data at the port level. Despite these issues, no better data source is available for our purposes, and the more highly aggregated BTS database is the standard source for trade flow statistics at northern border surface ports.

Data for the independent variables were obtained from source providers in the two countries. Canadian nominal GDP is from Statistics Canada, while U.S. nominal GDP is provided by the Bureau of Economic Analysis and was accessed through the FRED II database at the Federal Reserve Bank of St Louis. Daily values of the price of a U.S. dollar in Canadian cents were obtained from the FRED II database and were converted to quarterly frequency by averaging daily values.

Conclusions

In this chapter we identified and discussed a number of conceptual issues associated with statistically identifying the impact of 9/11 on bilateral trade. A critical issue in this regard is the necessary reliance on timing variables as proxies for the added explicit and implicit costs imposed on bilateral commercial shipments arising from security-related regulations and procedures in the post-9/11 time period. This indirect approach to identifying the linkage between 9/11 and bilateral trade raises a concern that other factors may be influencing trade flows and that their effects are being confounded with those arising from security responses to 9/11. This concern can be addressed, in part, by careful interpretation of the statistical results for the time variables, as well as by augmenting the statistical analysis with other investigations of industry and port-level developments in the post-9/11 time period.

6 The Aggregate Export and Import Equations

In this chapter we identify statistically a parsimonious specification of bilateral trade equations, which we then use to evaluate the impact of 9/11 on bilateral trade. The equation is initially 'calibrated' using data for the pre-9/11 period. The goal is to identify relatively simple U.S. export and import equations that are statistically reliable and then to incorporate time-period variables that allow the regression intercepts to differ between the pre- and post-9/11 periods. The estimated values of the time-period binary variables identify whether and how the bilateral trade relationship in the post- 9/11 period differs from the relationship in the pre-9/11 period.

Initial Estimation

In our initial U.S. import (Canadian export) equation, the dependent variable is specified as the natural log value of all Canadian exports to the United States expressed in billions of current U.S. dollars. One independent variable is the current (natural log) value of U.S. GDP.[1] A second is the Canada–U.S. exchange rate expressed as the number of Canadian dollars per U.S. dollar.[2] Specifying the GDP variable on a seasonally adjusted basis implicitly ignores demand-related seasonal factors influencing Canadian exports; moreover, there may be seasonal factors on the 'supply side' of product markets that create seasonality in Canada's exports to the United States. Hence, we also include three quarterly dummy variables in the estimating equation, with the first quarter of each year set to zero and each of the remaining three quarters taking values of zero or one as appropriate.

The initial version of the U.S. import equation over the period 1996Q1 through 2001Q2 was specified with the U.S. GDP variable lagged by one quarter and the exchange rate taking a contemporaneous value – that is, the value for the same quarter as the dependent variable. The GDP variable is initially lagged by one quarter in order to avoid any 'spurious' simultaneity problem with the dependent variable. Specifically, net exports are a component of real GDP. Larger imports will reduce the net export component of GDP, all other things constant, which in turn will lower measured GDP. The contemporaneous specification of the exchange rate is somewhat arbitrary in the absence of exogenous estimates of the 'optimal' exchange rate lag for overall Canadian exports to the United States. Indeed, given the importance of the U.S. market to Canada, a simultaneity problem may also exist between the dependent variable and the exchange rate. Since our specific concern is not to estimate an 'optimal' lag structure for the exchange rate, we have simply chosen to employ alternative specifications to find one or more statistically robust export equations. Lagged values from one through six quarters were chosen for the exchange rate. The estimating equations also include dummy variables for individual U.S. land ports of entry for imports from Canada. Specifically, individual variables were specified taking a value of unity for each of the ten largest land ports, with the remaining ports taking a value of zero.

Our expectation is that Canadian exports to the United States will be positively related to U.S. GDP, since Americans can be expected to purchase more of all types of products, including foreign-produced products, as their incomes rise. Furthermore, since both the export and GDP variables are measured in nominal U.S. dollar values, they will both increase as a result of inflation, which in turn contributes to a positive measured relationship between the two variables. The exchange rate variable should also be positively related to the dependent variable, since a higher value of the exchange rate as we measure it means that the Canadian dollar has depreciated against the U.S. dollar. A depreciated value of the Canadian dollar makes Canadian goods cheaper for U.S. importers, other things constant, which should encourage increased Canadian exports to the United States. Since seasonality patterns for U.S. imports from Canada are likely to vary by product, the likely signs for the seasonal dummy variables are difficult to predict, as they will reflect both the composition of Canadian exports in each quarter and the strengths of the seasonal patterns for the individual categories of commodities.

Descriptive statistics for the variables used in the trade equations are presented in Table 6.1. The results from estimating the equation for U.S. imports from Canada (Canadian exports to the U.S.) for alternative exchange rate lag structures are reported in Table 6.2. Specifically, model 1 is for the contemporaneous exchange rate specification. Models 2 through 7 involve lagging the exchange rate by one through six quarters, respectively. As can be seen, the expected positive sign for the exchange rate variable is realized for longer lag specifications, and the coefficients are statistically significant for the exchange rate variable lagged four through six quarters. The estimated equations with the longest lagged exchange rate values (five and six quarters) also tend to have marginally higher F-statistics, denoting somewhat better overall goodness of fits. This broad finding of a relatively long lag for the exchange rate's impact on Canadian exports is consistent with the previously discussed study by Ferley (2004). The latter found that a six-quarter lag on the exchange rate yielded the best statistical performance in the model for Canadian exports to the United States.

The seasonal adjustment coefficients are largely unaffected by the choice of exchange rate lag. They are uniformly statistically insignificant at acceptable (two-tailed) confidence levels. Conversely, the GDP coefficient is consistently statistically significant with the expected positive sign, although the size of the GDP coefficient, as well as its significance level, declines consistently moving from model 1 through model 7; however, the sizes of the GDP coefficients for the longer exchange rate lag specifications are more plausible than for the shorter lag specifications. The port dummies show that individual ports tend to be smaller than the aggregate residual category with the exception of the largest land port (Detroit).[3]

In summary, the parsimonious U.S. import (Canadian export) equation performs quite well statistically. The overall R-squared coefficients show that the equation is capable of 'explaining' most of the changes in U.S. imports from Canada over the sample period (the R-squared values are still high even if we control for port fixed effects, as will be seen in the next chapter where we examine port-level equations). The estimated coefficients for the main independent variables are generally statistically significant, with signs that are consistent with theoretical expectations. As such, the equation in chapter 5 (page

46) seems to provide a reasonable basis for examining the impact of post-9/11 developments on U.S. imports of Canadian products.

In a similar manner, we specify and estimate an equation for U.S. exports to Canada over the period 1997Q1 through 2001Q2.[4] In this case the 'income' variable is the natural log value of Canadian GDP expressed in current U.S. dollars. Higher values of Canadian GDP should encourage increased purchases of U.S. products. Given the specification of the exchange rate variable (i.e., number of Canadian currency units per U.S. dollar), we expect the estimated regression coefficient for the exchange rate variable to be negative in the U.S. export equation, since a depreciating Canadian dollar makes U.S. products more expensive for Canadians, other things constant. Again, in the absence of strong expectations about the 'optimal' lag for the exchange rate variable, we employ alternative lag specifications from zero to six quarters. The various model estimates are summarized in Table 6.3.

The estimation results for the U.S. export equation are not as satisfactory as for the U.S. import equation. Specifically, the exchange rate coefficient consistently has the incorrect sign, and moreover, it is statistically significant in all lag specifications. At the same time, the coefficient for the GDP variable is statistically insignificant in models 6 and 7. To be sure, the overall goodness of fit of the various models is quite high, as indicated by the R-squared and F coefficients. Hence, the parsimonious specification of the U.S. export equation appears to serve well as a 'forecasting' equation, although there are clearly problems with interpreting it as a reliable 'structural' explanation of U.S. exports to Canada.

As noted earlier, the models calibrated using pre-9/11 data and that are to serve as the basis for evaluating the stability of the bilateral trade regime in the post-9/11 period should be both structurally 'sensible' and econometrically robust. That is, the regression coefficients should be consistent with theoretical expectations and the overall and individual goodness-of-fit coefficients should be strong. The U.S. import equation satisfies both criteria, whereas the U.S. export equation satisfies the second but not the first criterion. It should be emphasized that our primary purpose is not to estimate a structurally sound trade model but, rather, to develop a reliable framework for evaluating whether and how the bilateral trade regime changed in the post-9/11 period. In this context, a statistically robust model might well be acceptable, albeit obviously less reliable than a model that meets both criteria.

Post-9/11 Trade Performance

The parsimonious equations described in Tables 6.2 and 6.3 were then respecified to test for the impact of post-9/11 developments associated with increased border security. Prior to doing so, we plotted overall U.S. imports from Canada and exports to Canada as a function of time. The plotted relationships are summarized in Figures 6.1 and 6.2. The objective of this exercise is to see whether there is any obvious graphical evidence of a change in the pattern of growth for U.S. imports and exports with Canada in the post-9/11 period. Since we are not explicitly holding the effects of other determinants of bilateral trade constant, such as changes in GDP values, the plotted relationships can be seen as suggestive, at best, of a '9/11 effect.' Nevertheless, the plots are indicative as to whether there is a possible 9/11 effect that might be identified through statistical estimation. The data summarized in the two figures show a downward movement in both imports and exports between 2001 and 2002, although the break is more evident in the case of U.S. imports from Canada.

To identify statistically whether there is a 9/11-related effect on overall bilateral trade, we effectively segment the sample into pre- and post-9/11 time periods. Specifically, dummy variables are introduced into each of the model equations reported in Tables 6.2 and 6.3. The individual time dummy variables are as follows: Yd01q3 takes a value of unity for 2001Q3 and zero otherwise; Yd01q4 takes a value of unity for 2001Q4 and zero otherwise; Yd02 through Yd04 take values of unity for years 2002 to 2004, respectively, and zero otherwise, while Yd05 takes a value of unity for 2005Q1 and zero otherwise. The precise specification of the time dummy variables is somewhat arbitrary inasmuch as it is not necessarily dictated by a priori expectations. Indeed, available information regarding waiting times and other possible indicators of security-related border disruptions is quite spotty, as noted in an earlier chapter. Hence, it seems advisable to adopt a general approach by allowing the presumed impacts of border security to vary fairly continuously over the post-9/11 period. We could have chosen to specify time dummy variables on a quarterly basis for the years 2002 to 2004, instead of specifying annual values; however, given the limited number of data points in the sample, this 'quarterly specification' would involve the loss of valuable degrees of freedom that in turn might compromise the efficiency of our estimation.

The results associated with including the time dummy variables in the U.S. import equation are reported in Table 6.4. Since the U.S. import (Canadian export) equations seem best specified with exchange rate lags of four to six quarters, the equations including the post-9/11 time dummies are reported for the exchange rate variable lagged four to six quarters. In fact, the broad pattern for the estimated time dummy coefficients is quite similar across all specifications of the exchange rate from contemporaneous to a six-quarter lag. For convenience, the coefficients for the port dummy variables are deleted; however, they are virtually identical to those reported in Table 6.2.[5]

The most salient result reported in Table 6.4 is the negative pattern of coefficients for the time dummy variables. Specifically, all of the time dummy coefficients are negative and statistically significant. Clearly, Canadian exports to the United States in the post-9/11 period were below what would have been expected, holding constant macroeconomic influences as well as seasonal effects. The pattern of the estimated coefficients is plausible, given the hypothesis that border disruptions related to post-9/11 security developments are the primary explanation for the fall-off in imports to the United States. Since most of 2001Q3 trade took place before 11 September, it is plausible that the impact of the border closing and slow reopening of the border on U.S. imports was stronger in the fourth quarter than in the third quarter of 2001. In fact, our results are consistent with that presumption, as the estimated coefficients for Yd01q4 are uniformly larger than those for Yd01q3. Efforts by the U.S. government to improve conditions at the border in early 2002 apparently had a modest impact, as the coefficient for the 2002 time dummy is slightly smaller than that for the 2001Q4 period. The negative border impact, then, apparently increased in 2003 and subsequently decreased through 2004 and early 2005.

The relative stability of the coefficients for the other included independent variables, most notably U.S. GDP and the exchange rate, when comparing results reported in Table 6.4 to those reported in Table 6.2, strengthens our confidence in the reliability of the estimating model underlying the equations reported in Table 6.4. The overall goodness-of-fit statistics for the equations in Table 6.4 are extremely strong, which lends additional confidence to our interpretation of the results, particularly our conclusion that post-9/11 developments have had a lingering adverse impact on Canadian exports to the United States.

As discussed in an earlier section of this study, a critical issue is whether the time sensitivity of Canadian exports to the United States can be confidently interpreted as reflecting security-related delays and other costs affecting cross-border commercial shipments, or whether other factors may be at work. Clearly, the continuous negative impact of time on Canadian export flows suggests that the relevant influences were not 'one-time' events but, rather, manifested their effects over the entire post-9/11 period, albeit with different intensities over that time period. The observed time-varying intensity itself suggests that the primary determinants are unlikely to reflect a phenomenon whose influence increases or decreases monotonically over time, such as growing shortages of truck drivers or capacity problems affecting rail carriers. Indeed, the pattern of the coefficients for the time dummy variables seems intuitively to fit a pattern dictated primarily by policies to address security and resulting congestion concerns at the border. We shall address this issue in more detail in a later chapter.

The primary inference that can be drawn from the results summarized in Table 6.4 is that the impacts of 9/11 and the subsequent enhanced security-related regulations and procedures continue to exert a negative influence on Canadian exports to the United States. The impacts for each time period can be evaluated by recognizing that the coefficient for each time dummy variable measures the relative decrease in exports.[6] For example, model 3 indicates that in 2001Q4, U.S. imports from Canada were around 20 per cent lower than they would have been in the absence of the border security consequences of 9/11. They were around 12 per cent lower in the first half of 2005 than they would otherwise have been.

The estimated coefficients for the time dummy variables represent the impact of security-related measures on exports for that year compared to the pre-9/11 period. Thus, the coefficient for the Yd05 variable shows that U.S. imports from Canada in the first half of 2005 were around 12 per cent lower than what would be expected from the experience over the period 1996Q1 through 2001Q2. Since the peak shortfall for Canadian exports was 2003, when Canadian exports were almost 26 per cent below the volume that would be expected based on pre-9/11 experience, the adverse impacts of border-related security developments have clearly been mitigated in recent years.

Our estimated U.S. import shortfalls are subject to at least two caveats. One is that they represent 'point estimates' that are midpoints of what is, statistically speaking, a confidence interval. This interval acknowledges a significant likelihood that the 'true' shortfall is less than the point estimated that we report. A second caveat is that our estimated shortfalls are relative to the import relationship that existed over the period 1996 through 2001Q2. If the import relationship was unusually strong for that period, then a portion of the estimated shortfall may reflect a return to a 'more normal' relationship.

The absolute decrease in U.S. imports from Canada can be calculated as follows. First, we use estimated model 1 in Table 6.4 to generate estimated values of imports from Canada in each of the time periods identified by our time dummy variables. Specifically, we multiply the values of the variables for each time period by the estimated coefficients for the variables to calculate fitted values for the dependent variable. We then recalculate fitted values for the dependent variable with the time dummy variables set equal to zero. In effect, the latter set of fitted values are the estimated imports from Canada had the effects of post-9/11 border security developments not been allowed to influence importing activity from Canada. Since the two fitted value series are in natural logs, antilogs were taken. The difference between the two series can then be interpreted as the shortfall in imports from Canada over the post-9/11 period presumably owing to enhanced border security.

The estimated shortfalls of U.S. imports from Canada in the post-9/11 period are summarized in Table 6.5. The estimated shortfalls are reported for each quarter beginning with 2001Q3 through 2005Q2. It should be noted that because Table 6.4 is a pooled (across ports) regression, the shortfalls reported in Table 6.5 represent the aggregated dollar value of import shortfalls from all ports expressed in millions of U.S. dollars. For example, total imports from Canada were almost US$12 billion less than they would otherwise have been during the 2005Q2 had 9/11 and the security responses to it not occurred.

Table 6.6 reports the estimation results for U.S. exports to Canada where the time dummy variables are included in the regression equation and results for the port dummies are not reported. Specifically, we report results for the exchange rate variable lagged one through four quarters.[7] In fact, the pattern of estimated coefficients for the time dummy variables is relatively unchanged across the different lag specifications for the exchange rate so that the estimated impact of time on U.S. exports is relatively insensitive to the precise lag specification chosen for the exchange rate.

The estimated pattern of coefficients for the time dummy variables indicates that the negative impact of post-9/11 developments on U.S. exports to Canada increased between 2001Q3 and 2001Q4 and then decreased consistently, at least for several of the lag specifications. In other cases, there is a very modest increase in 2003 followed by a consistent decrease. This was also more or less the pattern for the estimated time dummy coefficients for U.S. imports from Canada. One important apparent difference between the import and export equations is that the estimated coefficients for years 2004 and 2005 are statistically insignificant in the U.S. export equations, which suggests that border congestion effects had apparently 'disappeared' for northbound commercial shipments by the end of 2003. Conversely, statistically significant negative impacts on U.S. imports from Canada persisted through the 2005 period. In short, the 'conventional wisdom' that delays and related border disruptions have had larger adverse impacts on Canadian exporters than on U.S. exporters appears borne out by our results.

Table 6.7 summarizes the impacts on post-9/11 developments on U.S. exports to Canada. The impacts are estimated in an analogous manner to those reported in Table 6.5. Two clear differences emerge when the patterns of export shortfalls from Table 6.7 are compared with those for imports from Table 6.5. First, except for 2001Q3, the U.S. export shortfall is smaller than the import shortfall. Afterwards, imports are much more affected. The time pattern of the shortfalls is also quite different, with the export shortfalls largest in 2001Q4. The export shortfalls rise to almost the same level in 2003 but then are largely eliminated by 2005.[8] For imports, on the other hand, the shortfalls are still quite large in 2005.

Summary

Statistical analysis indicates that U.S. imports from Canada and exports to Canada were substantially and adversely affected by developments in the post-9/11 period. Our presumption is that the relevant developments are related to disruptions and increased costs imposed on shippers and manufacturers associated with enhanced border security procedures. While the adverse impacts on aggregate U.S. exports to Canada appear to have essentially disappeared by 2004, adverse impacts on U.S. imports from Canada have persisted at least through the first half of 2005.

7 Estimating Export and Import Equations at the Port Level

As mentioned earlier, an important focus of our study is to identify whether there are significant differences across major land ports in terms of the impacts of post-9/11 developments on bilateral trade. The identification of any such differences would obviously raise important questions about the reason(s) for the observed differences. It might also point towards policy initiatives that could help 'less successful' ports improve their performance with respect to processing commercial shipments.

Our approach towards identifying port-level differences in their post-9/11 experiences is to replicate the methodology implemented for aggregate exports and imports at the level of each of the ten largest land ports, as well as a residual category covering all other ports. Specifically, we estimate basic export and import equations at the individual port level. In doing so, we allow for differences across ports in the estimated coefficients for the basic variables identified in the aggregate export and import equations (i.e., GDP, the exchange rate, and the seasonal dummies). After estimating these basic equations, we introduce time dummy variables to capture the effects of post-9/11 developments on exports and imports at the level of the individual ports.

Port Level Estimation

The first extension of the basic trade equation specification is to estimate the parsimonious specification at the level of the individual port for the pre-9/11 time period. The objective is to identify whether a reliable specification can be identified at the individual port level in order to evaluate the impact of post-9/11 border disruptions on trade shipments on a port-by-port basis. Since a substantial number of ports are relatively small, we focused on the ten largest ports. Specifically, we estimated the same basic equations reported in Tables 6.2 and 6.3 for each of the following ports: (1) Highgate Springs; (2) Alexandria Bay; (3) Champlain–Rouses Point; (4) Buffalo–Niagara Falls; (5) Blaine; (6) Sweetgrass; (7) Pembina; (8) Portal; (9) Detroit; and (10) Port Huron.

The equations reported in Table 7.1 represent the 'best-performing' estimated equation for each port when the dependent variable is U.S. imports from Canada. The best-performing equation in this context equates to the specification of the lag value for the exchange rate variable that results in a correctly signed coefficient for the exchange rate variable with the highest estimated t-coefficient. For the most part, the coefficient estimates for the other included independent variables were not significantly altered by the precise lag structure chosen for the exchange rate variable. Moreover, the overall goodness-of-fit statistics were also largely unaffected by the specification chosen for the exchange rate lag. Hence, we do not believe that our results with respect to the impact of post-9/11 developments on Canadian exports to the United States are particularly sensitive to the precise specification of the exchange rate variable.

There are some clear differences across ports in the statistical results reported in Table 7.1. In particular, while the estimated coefficient for the exchange rate variable is fairly similar across the ten sample port equations, the estimated coefficient for the GDP variable differs noticeably across the individual port equations. Indeed, in the cases of Highgate Springs, Buffalo–Niagara Falls, and Detroit, the estimated GDP coefficients are not significantly different from zero at an acceptable confidence level. Similar differences can be identified for the seasonal adjustment dummy coefficients. As we discuss in detail in chapter 9, the commodity composition of trade differs across ports, and such differences may help account for differences in the estimated results across ports that are reported in Table 7.1. Specifically, commodities differ in terms of the response of imports from Canada with respect to GDP. Hence, differences in the mix of imports at the port level will likely contribute to differences in the estimated GDP coefficient.

Most of the estimated equations reported in Table 7.1 have relatively high overall R-squared and F coefficients, indicating that the equations 'explain' most of the variation in U.S. imports from Canada over the sample time period. The estimated coefficients for the GDP and exchange rate variables have their expected signs. Hence, for purposes of this study, it seems acceptable to proceed with using our parsimonious model to evaluate the impact of post-9/11 developments on U.S. imports of Canadian products.

We also estimate U.S. export (to Canada) equations for each of the ten largest ports. The results are reported in Table 7.2. Once again, for the sake of brevity, we report a single (best-performing) equation result for each port. It is clear that the U.S. export equations do not perform as well as the import equations. In particular, in about half the 'preferred' specifications, the estimated coefficient for the exchange rate variable has the incorrect (positive) sign, although in two of those cases the exchange rate variable is statistically insignificant. In addition, the overall goodness-of-fit statistics are uniformly lower in the export equations than in the import equations. In this respect, our estimation results for imports and exports at the individual port level are similar to those for aggregate imports and exports. Specifically, the import equations perform better than the export equations. Nevertheless, the export equations reported in Table 7.2 form the basis for evaluating the impact of 9/11 on U.S. exports to Canada.

The Impact of 9/11

In this section we explore the impact of 9/11 on bilateral exports and imports. By way of gaining a preliminary insight into the possible effect of security-related border disruptions, we graph the (natural log) values of imports from Canada to the United States and U.S. exports to Canada as a function of time for the full time period of our sample. We do this for each of the ten main ports in our sample, as well as graph exports and imports for a 'residual' port (i.e., all other ports).

Of particular interest is whether the graphs of exports and imports show any discrete 'break' in the third quarter of 2001, as well as how exports and imports behave after any observed break in the time series. While the graphical analysis does not hold other determinants of trade constant (besides time implicitly), if the border disruption effects of 9/11 and the security-related developments in its aftermath were severe, one might expect to see the value of exports and imports take a sharp and discrete drop at or around the third quarter of 2001 and perhaps stage a slow recovery from that point. Alternatively, if public and private-sector responses to the crisis were relatively effective in mitigating disruptions, one might expect to see a drop in exports and imports in the immediate aftermath of 9/11 followed by a relatively quick recovery to pre-9/11 volumes.

Appendix A provides the graphs of U.S. imports from Canada (quarterly sums of monthly values) for each of the 'eleven' ports. In virtually all cases, there was a decrease in U.S. imports from Canada in the immediate post-9/11 period. The rate at which trade growth resumed, as well as the extent of trade growth, varies across ports. For example, there is a fairly consistent, albeit 'saw-toothed' recovery of trade volumes for Blaine, whereas the recovery for Buffalo–Niagara Falls is somewhat delayed but sharp once it begins. Since we do not hold constant here other factors influencing trade volumes, notably U.S. GDP and the exchange rate, the graphs should not be interpreted as identifying the specific impacts of post-9/11 developments on trade flows; however, since U.S. GDP and the exchange rate are constants across the various ports, differences in pre- and post-9/11 trade flows across the sample of ports likely reflect port-specific differences. The graphs in Appendix A suggest that significant differences exist in the post-9/11 experience of our sample ports. The most obvious potentially relevant source of such differences across ports is the mix of commodities shipped. Another is access to rail transport.

Commodity Mix Differences across Ports

Appendix B reports the main commodity exports and imports cleared through the ten largest ports, as well as the residual 'all other' port category for two discrete periods: 2001Q2 and 2005Q2. Obvious and substantial differences in commodity mix can be identified for the various ports. For example, and unsurprisingly, road vehicles are overwhelmingly the main import from Canada, as well as the main export to Canada, cleared through the ports of Detroit and Port Huron. That category is also the single most prominent import and export crossing at the port of Buffalo–Niagara Falls. Electrical machinery accounts for the majority of imports and exports cleared through Highgate Springs, while non-ferrous metals is the single most important export and import shipped through the port of Alexandria Bay.

Other observations can be drawn from Appendix B. For example, road vehicles comprise a substantial share of shipments for many of the sample ports, reflecting the prominence of this industry in bilateral trade. Paper, paperboard, and related products are a prominent U.S. import from Canada for a number of ports, whereas various types of machinery are prominent U.S. exports to Canada through a number of different ports. While the precise distribution of imports and exports crossing through each sample port varies over the post-9/11 period, the changes are modest for the most part.

Regression Analysis of Post-9/11 Impacts at the Port Level[1]

As noted earlier, an important focus of our study is whether and how the impacts of post-9/11 border security developments vary across ports. We explore that issue here by re-estimating the parsimonious equations reported in Tables 6.4 and 6.6 for the ten largest individual ports in our sample, using the exchange rate lag specification for each port as reported in Tables 7.1 and 7.2.

Table 7.3 reports results for U.S. imports from Canada. Of particular interest is whether and how the coefficient estimates for the individual ports differ from those for other ports, particularly the coefficients for the time dummies. In this regard, the overall pattern of the estimated time dummy coefficients is fairly similar across ports, although Detroit and Buffalo–Niagara Falls are notable exceptions. Specifically, the smallest impact was typically experienced in 2001Q3. The impact increased in 2001Q4 and then remained fairly constant until either 2003 or 2004, when the negative impact on trade was the most pronounced for six of the ten ports. Highgate Springs, Sweetgrass, and Blaine are exceptions, inasmuch as they are the only three ports where the negative impact on trade in 2005 is absolutely larger than in 2004. The differences between 2004 and 2005 are small, however, except at Sweetgrass.

While the pattern of the coefficients for the time dummy variables is similar across ports, there are clear differences across ports in the magnitudes of the estimated coefficients associated with each time dummy variable. One might consider, for example, 2005. At one extreme, Canadian exports through the port of Detroit were actually higher in the first half of 2005 than would have been predicted by the parsimonious trade equation including GDP, the exchange rate, and the seasonal dummy variables. Specifically, the estimated coefficient for the 2005 dummy variable is positive and statistically significant. The coefficient suggests that Canadian exports were almost 22 per cent higher than would have been predicted, given standard determinants of U.S. imports from Canada based on the experience from 1996Q1 to 2001Q2.

At the other extreme, the Ports of Champlain–Rouses Point and Port Huron are characterized by substantially lower (and statistically significant) imports from Canada. In the cases of these two ports, imports in the first half of 2005 were on the order of 25 per cent below the levels that would be expected based on GDP, the exchange rate, and seasonal dummies. Reduced Canadian import levels of around 20 per cent are identifiable for the ports of Alexandria Bay, Portal, and Sweetgrass.[2] In the case of the port of Blaine, the 'shortfall' in imports from Canada in 2005 is around 13 per cent. Conversely, no statistically significant negative impact on Canadian exports can be identified for Highgate Springs, Buffalo–Niagara Falls, and Pembina. Thus, whereas all of the sample ports experienced a substantial and statistically significant reduction in Canadian imports at some point in the post-9/11 period, only about half the ports were still experiencing a significant negative impact by the first half of 2005.

In summary, six ports (Blaine, Champlain–Rouses Point, Port Huron, Alexandria Bay, Portal, and Sweetgrass) were still manifesting a significant reduction in Canadian exports to the United States through 2005Q2, whereas the other four large ports (Highgate Springs, Buffalo–Niagara Falls, Pembina, and Detroit) were not. It is beyond the scope of this study to attempt to explain these observed differences in any definitive way; however, in chapter 9 we briefly consider some possible explanations.

Table 7.4 reports the statistical results from estimating port-level U.S. export equations. One observation is that there is much greater variation in the pattern of estimated coefficients for the time dummy variables across ports than in the case of the equations reported for U.S. imports from Canada. For example, for some ports, the negative impact of post-9/11 developments decreases from 2003 to 2005, whereas for others it increases. Moreover, in the case of Detroit, none of the time dummy coefficients is statistically significant with a negative sign. Differences across ports with respect to the estimated coefficients for individual time periods are substantial. Again using 2005 as an example, U.S. exports to Canada through Sweetgrass were almost 41 per cent lower than they 'should' have been, whereas there was no statistically significant time period effect identified for Highgate Springs, Buffalo–Niagara Falls, Blaine, Portal, Detroit, and Port Huron. A statistically significant negative impact of around 25 per cent is identified for Alexandria Bay and around 15 per cent for Champlain–Rouses Point.

Summary

Statistical analysis shows that the impacts of border-related security developments are uneven across ports with respect to both U.S. imports and exports with Canada. Specifically, whereas trade volumes flowing through some ports have returned to levels consistent with pre-9/11 experience, others continue to suffer significant shortfalls from levels that might be expected based on conventional determinants of trade.

8 Interpreting the Estimated Impacts on Overall Bilateral Trade

In the preceding chapter we provided estimates of the 'shortfall' over time in U.S. trade with Canada that we attributed to security-related measures undertaken in the post-9/11 period. While the shortfalls for U.S. exports to Canada essentially disappeared by the middle of 2005, they persisted for U.S. imports from Canada. Moreover, the shortfalls in Canadian exports to the United States are relatively large, both in the aggregate as well as for individual border crossings. Indeed, our results suggest adverse impacts for Canadian exports that are much more serious than have been suggested by other studies, to date. It is, therefore, appropriate to evaluate whether other phenomena have adversely affected Canadian exports to the United States in the post-9/11 period that are not captured in our statistical model.

In this chapter we will assess other possible causes of changes in overall bilateral trade volumes in the post-9/11 period that are not explicitly considered in our empirical analysis. We also address why our estimated impacts on bilateral trade, particularly for U.S. imports from Canada, seem significantly larger than several other implicit estimates that have been suggested.

The Need to Consider Other Possible Trade Determinants

In an earlier chapter we noted a specific methodological concern with our approach to identifying the impacts of border security developments on bilateral trade. Namely, we relied on the estimated coefficients for our time dummy variables in order to identify the impacts of border-security related impediments to trade. To the extent that other factors influenced bilateral trade over our sample time period in the same way and with the same 'time profile' as our time dummy variables, we run the risk of mistakenly ascribing all observed shortfalls in trade flows to increased costs and disruptions associated with heightened border security rather than to other significant factors. As a result, our estimates of border security–related impacts on bilateral trade are likely to be overestimated.[1] It is therefore appropriate to assess whether factors other than enhanced border security measures might also account for the observed shortfall in trade identified by our time dummy variables within our parsimonious trade model.

Before undertaking any such evaluation, it is useful to summarize briefly the main trade shortfall patterns identified by our statistical analysis: (1) Commencing in 2001Q3, both U.S. imports from Canada and exports to Canada were lower than the values predicted by our trade equations. (2) The estimated trade shortfalls neither increased nor decreased monotonically over time. Rather, they decreased in relative terms in 2002, then increased and decreased over the remaining period. (3) By the end of the sample period, the estimated shortfall for U.S. imports from Canada was greater than the estimated shortfall for U.S. exports to Canada. Indeed, the U.S. export shortfall had, by and large, disappeared by the middle of 2005.

These observations have implications for any assessment of other possible determinants of our estimated trade shortfalls in the post-9/11 period. For example, potential determinants whose impacts are most plausibly 'constant' over the full sample period are unlikely to be a source of bias to our estimated time dummy coefficients. A possible example in this regard is traffic congestion associated with a growth in trade volumes that exceeded the expansion of transportation infrastructure, particularly in border communities. Concerns about traffic congestion had been expressed long before 9/11, and the relatively dramatic gap between 'expected' and actual trade that emerged after 9/11 cannot plausibly be linked to a significant contraction in the capacity of the transportation infrastructure to facilitate bilateral trade.

Similarly, factors that can be expected to have roughly equivalent impacts on U.S. imports and exports are unlikely to be potential determinants of the estimated trade shortfalls that are not explicitly included in our model. A possible example here is the price of fuel. Commercial shippers experienced significant increases in fuel costs in 2004 and 2005. To the extent that these increased costs were passed through to customers, some substitution of domestic purchasing for foreign buying could be expected that, in turn, might be manifested in smaller trade flows than would otherwise be expected; however, any such impact should be apparent both for U.S. imports and U.S. exports, with no reason to expect that the impact would be stronger and longer-lasting for U.S. imports.

Clearly, there are numerous possible alternative explanations of the observed trade shortfalls identified in our econometric estimation. One can adopt a purely 'deductive' approach to evaluating the potential explanations. That is, one might evaluate the relevance of the potential explanations against the background of the observed pattern of the estimated time dummy variable coefficients. With no screening of the potential explanations ex ante, however, this approach is likely to be impractical. Simply put, there are clearly many influences on bilateral trade that are not captured explicitly in our model, and to identify and assess the plausibility of each influence as a possible cause of observed trade shortfalls is well beyond the scope of any individual study or set of studies.

An alternative approach is more 'inductive.' Specifically, one might focus on the categories of trade that are quantitatively important in the bilateral context with the following question in mind: Were there any developments in the post-9/11 period unrelated to border security that might contribute to the trade shortfall pattern identified by our statistical model for the specific industry in question? In addressing this question to the major industries accounting for bilateral trade, one is effectively evaluating the issue for aggregate bilateral trade flows.

As noted in chapter 3, U.S. imports from Canada are relatively concentrated in the following sectors: transportation equipment, particularly motor vehicles and parts; energy, including oil and gas and petroleum products; forest products; and fabricated metals. Hence, to assess the reliability of our interpretation of the time dummy variable coefficients, we investigate whether other post-9/11 developments in these major sectors might account for bilateral trade shortfalls, particularly with respect to U.S. imports from Canada.

Transportation Equipment

At issue in the case of transportation equipment, as in the other sectors to be assessed, is whether factors other than economic growth, exchange rate movements, and border security developments could have contributed to a substantial shortfall in bilateral trade, particularly U.S. imports from Canada, below levels that would have otherwise been expected in the post-9/11 period. An obvious potential factor is an increase in trade on the part of Canada and the United States with other countries that substituted for trade between the two countries. For example, if both countries increased imports of assembled vehicles and parts from the rest of the world while reducing imports of those products from each other, bilateral trade could be expected to decline. Furthermore, to the extent that the substitution in favour of equipment produced outside of Canada and the United States was not directly related to changes in GDP in the two countries, or to the Canada–U.S. exchange rate, this development could contribute to the observed trade shortfall identified by our model.

The broadest potential factor to consider in this regard is whether the 'competitiveness' of transportation equipment companies in the United States, and, particularly, Canada in light of our statistical findings, deteriorated relative to foreign rivals in the post-9/11 period. If this were the case, one might expect offshore imports of parts and assembled products to displace North American production. Given the degree to which the Big Three automakers in North America have integrated production across their facilities in Canada and the United States, reduced production activity for the Big Three is likely to be associated with a reduction in bilateral trade (Studer 2004).

The available evidence suggests that the Japanese competitive challenge to the Big Three North American–based auto companies continued in the post-9/11 period (ibid., 2004); however, the competitive challenge was manifested not so much in terms of offshore imports of assembled vehicles and parts, but rather in increased sales by foreign producers with plants in North America, particularly the Japanese manufacturers.[2] The phenomenon of foreign direct investment in the North American auto industry reflects two main factors. One is NAFTA's domestic rules-of-origin requirements, which oblige producers to meet a 62.5 per cent North American value-added content requirement if they hope to export assembled vehicles within North America duty free. Such rules of origin encourage foreign firms to establish production facilities in North America, given tariffs on imports that do not qualify as North American–made products. A second is the voluntary export restrictions that Japan adopted in deference to U.S. political pressure against growing Japanese auto exports. These restrictions also encouraged Japanese car manufacturers to establish assembly and parts facilities within North America.

The growth of motor vehicle sales from production facilities of foreign transplants is suggested by data reported in Table 8.1. The data suggest that the market share for foreign vehicles made in North America increased fairly consistently from 1995 through the first nine months of 2004. For passenger cars, the market share was 24.2 per cent in 2000, increasing to 30.9 per cent in 2004. Similarly for trucks, the market share was 6.4 per cent in 2000, increasing to 9.2 per cent in 2004.

The displacement of Big Three production by foreign transplants could possibly reduce cross-border trade in vehicles and parts to the extent that transplants engage in less intra-industry trade per dollar of final sales than do production units owned by the Big Three companies. Firm-level data on intra-industry trade are unavailable; however, data for the auto industry as whole, reported in Table 8.2, do not suggest a substantial change in overall intra-industry trade between Canada and the United States for the period 1997 to 2004.[3] Specifically, intra-industry trade between Canada and the United States increased for the parts segment and was virtually unchanged for the assembly and body segments. The data in the table therefore suggest that cross-border trade in the auto sector between Canada and the United States should not have been adversely affected by less cross-border 'contracting out' of production by firms in the industry.

Available information also does not support arguments that Canadian producers were less efficient than their U.S. counterparts such that more production took place in the U.S. and less in Canada, thereby contributing to the identified shortfall in Canadian exports to the United States. Rather, the reverse seems to be the case. One report identifies Canada enjoying a 1 per cent productivity advantage in car assembly compared to the U.S. in the mid-1990s. This advantage is estimated to have increased to 5 per cent in 2000 and to around 7 per cent by 2002 (Collins 2002). A KPMG study for 2004 ranked eleven countries on the basis of automotive production costs. Canada ranked second behind Australia, while the United States ranked fifth.

In sum, there is no strong support for concerns that changes in international competitiveness may have led to Canada being a less desirable location for the production of automotive products in the post-9/11 period. Beyond any exchange rate advantage, Canadian producers enjoyed a productivity advantage over U.S.-based producers – an advantage that apparently increased in the post-9/11 period. This condition is inconsistent with our finding of a significant shortfall of Canadian exports to the U.S. that persisted through mid-2005, whereas any shortfall of U.S. exports to Canada had essentially disappeared by 2004.

Oil, Gas, and Petroleum Products

As in the case of transportation, the relevant issue here is whether changes in bilateral trade flows in oil, natural gas, and petroleum products in the post-9/11 period took place that are not explicitly included in our statistical model or that are not acknowledged in our interpretation of the model's results. We are particularly concerned with the possibility that Canadian exports in these areas may have declined in the post-9/11 period for reasons unrelated to border security arrangements, thereby contributing to a decrease in overall Canadian exports to the United States that we, in turn, attribute to border security developments.

Given that oil and gas are primarily transported by pipeline, it is extremely unlikely a priori that any decline in Canadian exports in these products could be attributable to border security–related developments. Hence, any significant decrease in oil and gas exports from Canada to the United States in the post-9/11 period that are unrelated either to changes in GDP or to the exchange rate should not mistakenly be attributed to events directly linked to 9/11. On the other hand, tanker trucks are an important source of transport for petroleum products, and therefore might be adversely affected by border crossing disruptions.

In the context of bilateral energy trade, the prices of oil and natural gas are potentially important influences on the nominal (dollar) value of U.S. imports (and exports). Specifically, a significant decrease in the prices of oil and natural gas in the post-9/11 period would contribute to a reduction in energy exports and imports, other things constant, since the demand for energy inputs is price inelastic.[4] Another, albeit less likely, possibility is that offshore imports of energy became more attractive to North American buyers post-9/11, particularly to buyers who were importing energy from Canada.

The potential for a decrease in unit prices to significantly depress measured values of bilateral exports of oil and natural gas post-9/11 can be relatively quickly dismissed. The average nominal price of crude oil in the United States was around US$27.40 in 2000. It decreased to $23 in 2001 and then decreased marginally to $22.80 in 2002; however, it increased sharply thereafter to $27.69 in 2003, $37.66 in

2004, and $50.04 in 2005. The price of U.S. natural gas pipeline imports from Canada (U.S. dollars per thousand cubic feet) increased from $3.97 in 2000 to $4.43 in 2001. It then decreased to $3.13 in 2002, only to increase to $5.23 in 2003 and $5.80 in 2004. During the first half of 2005, the price fluctuated between $6 and $7.[5] Given that petroleum products are derived from crude oil, price changes for petroleum products can be expected to change in the same direction as crude oil prices, and that, in fact, was the case. Specifically, an index of petroleum product prices increased consistently from 2002 to 2005 after declining slightly in 2001 and in 2002.

A shift in buying preferences of U.S. importers away from North American sources of energy cannot be dismissed as a possible contributor to reduced exports from Canada to the United States that is not identified either explicitly or implicitly by our model. Specifically, physical units of natural gas imports from Canada into the United States as a share of total natural gas imports by the United States averaged around 94 per cent from 2000 to 2002; however, this share declined to around 87 per cent in 2003 and to around 85 per cent in 2004. The decline appears to be due to more rapid growth in offshore imports of liquefied natural gas. Imports of crude oil from Canada in physical units accounted for almost 15 per cent of total U.S. imports of crude oil in 2000. This share decreased slightly, to approximately 14.5 per cent in 2001, but increased to 15.8 per cent in 2002 and to 16 per cent in both 2003 and 2004. On balance, therefore, there was relatively little change in the share of U.S. crude oil imports accounted for by Canada. U.S. imports of petroleum and natural gas products from Canada (in equivalents of barrels of oil) declined from around 19.2 per cent in 2000 to 18.6 per cent in 2001. They then increased to 22 per cent in 2002, only to decline to 20.1 per cent in 2003 and to 17.1 per cent in 2004.

In summary, there are grounds for concern that decreases in Canada's share of U.S. energy imports, particularly in natural gas and petroleum products, may account for some of the shortfall of U.S. imports from Canada in the post-2001 period. The observed decreases in Canada's share of U.S. energy imports cannot plausibly be tied to border security developments, since natural gas and a portion of petroleum products are transported to the United States via pipeline, and security-related disruptions are not particularly relevant to pipeline shipments. Hence, we must acknowledge the possibility that our estimates of shortfalls of Canadian exports to the United States in the post-2001 period are overstated owing to the substitution of off-shore imports for Canadian imports, at the margin.

Metals and Metal Products

As in the case of oil, oil products, and natural gas, the measured value of North American trade in metals and metal products might be affected either by changes in the average prices of those products or because shipments of those products from other countries displace shipments from either Canada to the U.S. or from the U.S. to Canada for reasons that are unrelated to factors captured by our model.

The wide variety of minerals and metal products makes it difficult to evaluate a single index of prices to assess the potential relevance of changes in underlying prices as a cause of our estimated trade short-falls; however, price indices are readily available for a number of metals that are the basis for most of Canada's exports of fabricated metal products.[6] Specifically, we identified the annual index of prices for aluminum, copper, nickel, lead, and zinc over the period 2000 to 2004 with the year 2000 as the base year. While not identical, there is some similarity in the movement of the price indices of the different metals. Specifically, with the exception of nickel, the price indices declined from 2000 to 2002. They then increased consistently from 2002 to 2004. Indeed, the increases between 2003 and 2004 were quite substantial, ranging from a low of 20 per cent for aluminum to a high of 72 per cent for lead. These data suggest that decreases in metal prices cannot plausibly account for any observed trade shortfalls identified by our model for the post-2002 period. Moreover, prices for copper were virtually unchanged between 2001 and 2002 and actually increased between those two years in the case of nickel, casting further doubt on the empirical relevance of metal price changes as a source of the identified trade shortfall in the post-2001 period.

Forest Products

A potentially important development in Canada–U.S. trade relations is the softwood lumber dispute. This trade conflict has been ongoing since 1982, when Congress directed the International Trade Commission to begin an investigation of Canadian and U.S. lumber producers in response to claims by U.S. producers that the Canadian government was subsidizing its domestic industry through the non-competitive allocation of timber.[7] It is beyond the scope of this chapter to review the long history of the dispute and the resulting U.S. government actions. Suffice to say that duties were imposed by the United States on softwood lumber exports from Canada in 1992. A five-year agreement was reached between the two countries in 1996 whereby British Columbia was allowed to export up to 9 billion board feet of softwood lumber annually without penalty, with graduated fees imposed for shipments over certain limits. Alberta, Ontario, and Quebec agreed to raise their stumpage fees and also faced financial penalties for exports above stated limits.

The Softwood Lumber Agreement expired in March 2001. Government data showed that shipments of softwood lumber from Canada to the United States increased nearly 50 per cent from March to April. From the first to the second quarter of 2001, shipments increased almost 20 per cent. At the same time, lumber prices for exports were quite strong, increasing by around 66 per cent between January and May of 2001. The U.S. Department of Commerce levied a 19 per cent preliminary countervailing duty against lumber imports from Canada in August 2001. Canadian producers increased their quoted prices by around 20 per cent in order to cover the countervailing duty; however, weak sales in response to the price increase forced Canadian producers to adjust quoted prices downwards. A preliminary finding in October 2001 required Canadian producers to post bonds to cover an antidumping duty of 12.6 per cent in addition to the earlier countervailing duty. In April 2002 the Department of Commerce announced that the final countervailing duty rate would be lowered from 19.3 to 18.8 per cent, while the antidumping duty would be lowered from 9.7 per cent to 8.4 per cent. Under pressure from NAFTA tribunal decisions, the Department of Commerce further lowered the countervailing duty and antidumping rates to 17.2 per cent and 4 per cent in December 2004.

A possible implication of the softwood dispute and the subsequent actions undertaken by the U.S. government is that the prices received by Canadian exporters and/or the volumes of wood exported by Canadian companies may have decreased dramatically commencing in 2001 in response to the duties imposed by the U.S. government on those shipments. Moreover, the imposition of the duties as a replacement for the Softwood Lumber Agreement might well contribute to the observed persistence of the observed shortfall in Canadian exports to the United States in the post-9/11 period. In this regard, the chronology of disincentives to Canadian wood export values created by U.S. government initiatives overlap the time series dummies in our model, thereby raising a concern that our dummy time variable measures might be 'picking up' the effects of government actions against Canada's lumber industry rather than security-related border disruptions.

In fact, lumber prices declined in 2001 and 2002, as did other commodity prices, as noted above. It is unclear how much of the decrease in prices was associated with the actions of the U.S. government and how much was the consequence of the North American recession in 2000–1. In any case, lumber prices rallied strongly in the summer of 2003 in response to a strong upturn in U.S. housing construction, as did prices for wood-based panels. The continued strength of the U.S. housing market in 2004 supported additional price increases in lumber and wood-based panels in 2004 (Natural Resources Canada 2004); however, lumber and wood product prices were lower in the first half of 2005 compared to the first half of 2004. Prices of newsprint and pulp followed a pattern that was not dissimilar to that of lumber and wood products. Specifically, prices for those commodities declined through 2001 and 2002, but then increased in 2003 and 2004, only to decrease again in 2005.

The decreases in forest product prices in 2001 and 2002 might contribute to the observed shortfall of Canadian exports to the U.S. in those years, although it should be noted that the largest part of the decline in prices occurred in the first half of 2001. At the same time, the sharp increase in prices should have mitigated any observed export shortfall in 2003 and 2004. In sum, it is not possible to dismiss unequivocally the relevance of lower forest product prices as a contributor to the Canadian export shortfall estimated by our model, at least for specific years. On the other hand, the fact that prices, particularly for lumber, were quite strong for several post-9/11 years mitigates against forest product prices being a strong source of bias over the entire post-9/11 period for our sample.

It must also be acknowledged that the countervailing and antidumping duties imposed by the U.S. government might well have kept physical volumes of Canadian lumber below what they would otherwise have been in the post-9/11 period. In this regard, the volume of Canadian softwood lumber exports to the United States actually increased in 2003 and 2004, reflecting strong U.S. housing construction, and Canada's share of the U.S. softwood lumber market was relatively stable from 2002 to 2004 (Natural Resources Canada 2004). In any case, a decrease in softwood lumber exports is unlikely to be a major source of bias to our estimated Canadian export shortfalls, as less than 3 per cent of Canada's total commodity exports to the U.S. are compromised of softwood lumber (Government of British Columbia 2005).

Summary

In summary, our relatively brief assessment of possible post-9/11 developments affecting major bilateral trading sectors, particularly from the perspective of Canadian exports to the United States, does not provide strong grounds for concern that we have unwittingly overlooked major factors contributing to estimated trade shortfalls while ascribing the consequences of those factors to increased border security and its associated costs. To be sure, it is quite possible that estimates of trade shortfalls in the period immediately after 9/11 exaggerate the impacts of enhanced border security, because our model does not explicitly identify the possible negative impact of the 2000–1 recession on commodity prices;[8] however, the strong recovery in commodity prices in 2003 and 2004 mitigates this concern for the later years in our sample.

It is also possible that trade disagreements, most notably involving softwood lumber but also affecting grain and meat exports from Canada, may have led to reductions in exports from Canada in the post-2001 period in ways not explicitly captured by our model. Nevertheless, given the small share these products have in Canada's overall exports to the United States, it is unlikely that this omission is a substantial contributor to any overestimate of the impacts of border-related security disruptions on bilateral trade.

On balance, we must acknowledge the likelihood that our estimated impacts of border security on trade flows are higher than the 'true' impacts. Supporting this caveat is the observation that our estimates are significantly above those implied by the findings of Lee and her colleagues (2005). It should be recalled that these authors conclude that border security developments have led to reduced exports from Quebec to the United States, although the reduction is probably less than 2 per cent of 2004 exports. When applied to Canada's total exports, our impact estimate is five to six times the size of their estimate.

A full evaluation of possible reasons for the discrepancy between our estimates and those of Lee and her colleagues is beyond the scope of this study. As noted above, one possible reason is that our statistical results overestimate Canadian export shortfalls for reasons given earlier. Another possible reason is that Lee and her colleagues do not allow for the possibility that border disruptions and related uncertainties adversely affected the just-in-time production and delivery systems of North American firms such that some increased intra-industry trade that might otherwise have taken place, did not. Equivalently, they assume that all border security–related costs are direct and completely passed on to consumers. If some costs are borne by firms – say, in the form of reduced efficiency – the impact may not only be in higher prices and reduced purchases by foreign buyers, but also in forgone production increases which would, in turn, be manifested as estimated trade shortfalls in our models. In the next chapter we assess trade shortfall patterns by port. This analysis may shed additional light on whether our trade shortfall estimates exclude the possible influence of other intervening determinants.

9 Interpreting the Estimated Impacts at Individual Ports

In chapter 7 we identified differences in estimated trade shortfalls across main surface ports in the United States. These differences have potentially significant policy implications. In particular, they suggest that initiatives to improve the flow of commercial shipments, particularly shipments from Canada to the United States where aggregate trade shortfalls are most significant, might be more effective if they were concentrated on those ports where post-9/11 trade shortfalls are still persisting. In this chapter we look more closely at the estimated trade shortfalls at the individual port level, to try to assess the reliability of our findings as well as to identify potential policies to address the border-related security problems at the specific ports where they seem most significant.

Commodity Differences

While there is presumably more than one potential cause of the observed differences in trade shortfalls by port, different commodity compositions of imports might be part of the explanation, either because certain goods are more prone to border delays, as suggested by Goldfarb and Robson (2003), or because specific shippers were better than others in responding to increased delays and variable waiting times. In this regard, it is potentially relevant to note that in the case of three of the four ports for which no statistically significant reduction in imports from Canada could be identified for 2005 compared with the pre-9/11 period, road vehicles were the single largest import category.[1] It may well be that auto manufacturers in North America were better able than other shippers to coordinate responses to border delays and disruptions. To be sure, however, road vehicles are also the single largest import through Port Huron, the port that exhibits significant reduced imports from Canada through 2005.

In considering the potential influence of commodity differences, it is useful to segment the large U.S. ports in terms of the statistical magnitudes of the estimated trade shortfalls. For convenience, we consider the estimated trade shortfalls as of the first half of 2005. The signs and the levels of statistical significance for the Yd05 coefficients reported in Table 7.3 suggest that the large sample ports can be divided into three categories: (1) Those where no statistically significant trade shortfall is identified as persisting through 2005Q2. This set includes Buffalo–Niagara Falls, Pembina, and Detroit. (2) Those where a negative impact persists, although the Yd05 coefficient is marginally statistically significant. This set includes Highgate Springs and Sweetgrass. (3) Those where a negative and highly significant Yd05 coefficient is identified. This set includes Champlain–Rouses Point, Blaine, Portal, and Port Huron.

The commodity composition of imports from Canada cleared through the various ports was reported in Appendix B. For the three ports that exhibit no significant import shortfall from Canada by 2005, road vehicles are the leading import category. In the cases of Buffalo–Niagara Falls and Detroit, road vehicles' share of total imports is substantial. In the case of Pembina, the distribution of commodities is more even, and road vehicles are a relatively small share of total imports for that port. While there are overlapping categories of commodities for the three ports, such as paper products, the overlapping categories are relatively small shares of the total imports passing through the three ports.

Looking at the four ports exhibiting the largest import shortfalls through 2005Q2, there are substantial differences in the commodity shipment compositions for the individual ports. For example, road vehicles are, by a wide margin, the largest single import category in the case of Port Huron. Road vehicles are a much smaller share of total imports for the ports of Blaine, Champlain–Rouses Point, and Portal. The leading imports for these latter three ports differ, although cork and wood is a large category in the cases of Blaine and Portal; however, cork and wood is a relatively small import category for Champlain–Rouses Point. Special transactions and commodities are relatively large import categories for Champlain–Rouses Point and Blaine, but they are relatively small categories in the cases of Portal and Port Huron.

Comparing the ports of Highgate Springs and Sweetgrass, there are substantial differences in commodity shares. For example, while meat and meat preparations is the largest share of imports in the case of Sweetgrass, it is not represented in the case of Highgate Springs. Conversely, electrical machinery is, by far, the major import category for Highgate Springs. It is not represented in the case of Sweetgrass. Among the five largest (by share) commodity imports for the two ports, only special transactions and commodities are represented for both ports.

In sum, there is no obvious pattern linking the distribution of commodity shipments to the magnitude of the import shortfall across the ten leading surface ports. There is some indication that the ports that were experiencing no import shortfall by 2005Q2 were intensively involved in shipping motor vehicles; however, motor vehicles were the largest import category for Port Huron, and it exhibited a relatively large import shortfall that persisted through the end of our sample time period. It would therefore seem reasonable to conclude that port differences in import shortfalls are not primarily a reflection of differences in the mix of commodities shipped through the ports. Rather, the port differences identified may reflect differences across ports in their responses to increased border security imperatives.

Infrastructure Differences

Another potential candidate to explain differences across ports in estimated trade shortfalls is infrastructure, that is, the infrastructure conditions characterizing those ports. In particular, differences in ease of access to inspection facilities at individual ports, as well as differences in the capacities and efficiencies of the inspection facilities themselves, might help explain observed differences across ports in the estimated impacts of 9/11 on trade shortfalls.[2] That such differences exist is entirely plausible; however, in the context of this study, it was not possible to do a detailed port-by-port evaluation of the relevant conditions.

Perhaps the most striking difference observed across the U.S. land ports in our study involves the experience of Port Huron relative to those of Detroit and Buffalo–Niagara Falls, particularly given the concentration of motor vehicle shipments through all three ports. While the estimated trade shortfalls in the first two quarters following 9/11 were apparently greater for Buffalo–Niagara Falls and Detroit than for

Port Huron, the opposite was the case between 2003 and 2005. The inference one might draw from this observation is that border crossing conditions at the time of 9/11 for specific ports were not determinative of border crossing conditions throughout our sample period. That is, congestion and related problems apparently got worse in locations such as Port Huron relative to locations such as Buffalo–Niagara Falls and Detroit. The issue is why.

Observers have cited the existence of border crossing congestion problems prior to 9/11, and those problems apparently were relevant for all major border crossings (Center for Automotive Research 2002).[3] Congestion at the approach aprons was the most frequently mentioned cause of border-related delays. The root cause of the congestion is often traced, primarily on the U.S. side, to inadequate staffing at border crossings (ibid.). It is therefore possible that staffing levels at Port Huron were less adequate, given the increased security demands, than at other major ports such as Detroit and Buffalo–Niagara Falls, although we have no direct evidence bearing on this hypothesis. It is also possible that border security procedures were unevenly applied from port to port. In this regard, the Center for Automotive Research (2002, 18) reports inconsistent handling of inspections and paperwork at various port crossings, although it also notes that the largest suppliers and trucking operations did not see this as a problem.

One notable and documentable difference between Port Huron and other major ports is the significantly higher share of shipments carried by rail rather than by truck through the Port Huron crossing. For example, in 2002 around 84 per cent of the value of goods shipped through the port of Detroit was shipped by truck. In contrast, only about 57 per cent of the value of goods shipped through Port Huron arrived by truck. Bonsor (2004) discusses the particular problems that security inspections can impose on rail shipments, particularly for goods shipped by rail from Canada to the United States. Specifically, when U.S. Customs wants to physically examine a container on a train, the container has to be removed from the train. This means that the railcar has to be removed from the train and the container from the railcar. The procedure (especially with high-capacity, double-stack cars) can take several hours, and if the container is not inspected on site, it has to be trucked to a warehouse for inspection. This not only causes considerable delay to the train being inspected but also contributes to a backlog of other trains. Hence, while a relatively small percentage of containers are apparently subjected to physical inspection, the adverse impact on shipments can be quite severe.[4]

The concentration of rail shipments through Port Huron might also partly explain our statistical findings of persisting trade shortfalls through that port compared to its counterparts in Detroit and Buffalo–Niagara Falls. It is intrinsically more difficult to expand rail capacity in the short run than it is to add trucking capacity. Significant expansion of rail capacity might oblige the rail companies to invest in new rail lines and yards, while trucking companies can acquire a few additional trucks and drivers. This phenomenon is potentially quite relevant, given the relatively rapid growth in traffic using the Blue Water Bridge connecting Canada to the United States through Port Huron. Indeed, the Blue Water Bridge was apparently the fastestgrowing Canada–U.S. commercial crossing over the period 1993 to 2002.[5] To be sure, the problem of railway capacity expansion is not necessarily related to increased border security, although major investments in fixed and sunk cost physical capital can be discouraged, at the margin, by uncertainties regarding future regulatory procedures such as those related to border security requirements.[6]

It is interesting to note that other ports experiencing significant and persisting import shortfalls in the post-9/11 period are also characterized by relatively intensive use of rail shipments. In particular, relatively high percentages of total shipments through Portal and Blaine are carried by rail. The potential relevance of mode of transport to post-9/11 import shortfalls is underscored by graphs of trucking's share of total shipments of imports and exports as reported in Appendix C.

Conclusions

We are not able to offer any definitive explanations of the observed differences across ports in estimated trade shortfalls; however, we are prepared to venture the opinion that the observed differences are not primarily a consequence of differences in the commodity composition of shipments going through each port. Rather, the differences more likely reflect differences in conditions surrounding the nature of port infrastructure, as well as in the procedures that are followed at individual ports. This, in turn, suggests that focused investments and changes in procedure at the level of individual ports can be effective means to mitigate border crossing problems.

10 Potential Impacts on Capital Investment

The preceding two chapters presented some evidence bearing on the possibility that our statistical estimates of the impacts of 9/11 on bilateral trade flows might be overstated because they fail to adequately account for other influences on trade flows in the post-9/11 period besides those related to border security developments. The evidence suggests that any upward bias is likely to be modest and that our broad conclusions with respect to the linkage between bilateral trade and post-9/11 security developments are quite plausible.

In this chapter we consider whether post-9/11 security developments have affected investment patterns in North America. In particular, we evaluate the hypothesis that capital investment in Canada has been discouraged relative to capital investment in the United States. The perception of observers, which is supported by our statistical results, is that Canadian shipments to the United States have been more 'disadvantaged' by post-9/11 developments than have shipments from the United States to Canada. A possible consequence of this asymmetry is that some U.S. importers of Canadian products have switched their sourcing of those products from Canadian exporters to local producers. Indeed, the switching away of sourcing from Canadian exporters to U.S.-based producers might underlie, at least in part, the export shortfall from Canada to the United States identified in this study.

The resulting expansion of production in the United States and reduction of production in Canada should ultimately be paralleled in increased capital investment in the United States relative to capital investment in Canada, holding other factors constant. In particular, multinational companies in North America might relocate some production from Canada to the United States in order to mitigate disruptions to their North American supply chains. Furthermore, in order to facilitate increased production in the United States relative to Canada, the multinational companies might be expected to expand their production facilities in the United States relative to those in Canada.

The distribution of foreign direct investment (FDI) flows in North America might be seen as an important indicator of the attractiveness of Canada as a location for international production activity relative to the United States. In principle, if one were interested in the factors influencing foreign direct investment flows into and from Canada and the United States, one would specify and estimate statistical equations in which FDI inflows and outflows were dependent variables, and the primary factors influencing those inflows and outflows were independent variables.[1] This formal statistical approach is beyond the scope of this study. Rather, we rely on a broad examination of FDI patterns, in conjunction with explanations of those patterns found in the literature.

Recent Patterns of Foreign Direct Investment

A basic problem with simply looking at FDI flows over time is that they are likely to be influenced by a number of factors. One of the main factors influencing inward FDI is the overall size of the host economy. Foreign investors prefer to establish and expand foreign affiliates in relatively large host economies for two main reasons. One is that a relatively large host economy provides greater demand for the goods and services produced in foreign affiliates in that economy. A second is that relatively large economies, particularly developed countries, usually possess an array of diverse resources and skills that, in turn, promote what economists call 'external economies of scale.' The latter, also sometimes called 'agglomeration economies' are efficiency gains in production and distribution activities that arise from the greater degree of specialization of the workforce, and the faster diffusion of new technology, that characterizes larger markets.[2]

Empirical studies find that a measure of the overall size of the host country market is the strongest single explanatory variable in statistical models of FDI inflows. One such measure of overall size is the GDP of the host country. Hence, FDI inflows as a ratio of host country GDP are a suggestive indicator of the attractiveness of the host country as a location for international production. Similarly, FDI outflows as a ratio of home country GDP are potentially indicative of disadvantages suffered by the home country relative to other countries as a location for international production.

Before presenting any data, it is useful to define terms. Gross inflows of foreign direct investment include investments originating outside the host country that are made by foreigners in host country businesses in which the foreign investor plays an active management role plus earnings that are reinvested in the host country by foreign-owned affiliates in that country. Gross outflows include investments made by home country investors in actively managed businesses located in foreign countries plus earnings that are repatriated by foreign-owned affiliates in the home country.

Globerman and Shapiro (2003), among others, document the volatility of FDI inflows and outflows on a year-to-year basis. Hence, it is prudent to report inward and outward foreign investment ratios averaged over subperiods. In this regard, Table 10.1 reports ratios of inward and outward FDI to GDP for Canada and the United States over different subperiods since 1990 expressed as percentages. Looking first at the ratio of inward FDI to GDP, it is seen that the ratio for Canada increased substantially in the second half of the 1990s compared to the first half. It should be noted that the increase is heavily influenced by a dramatic increase in inward FDI in 2000. If the ratio of inward FDI to GDP is recalculated for the period 1995 to 1999 and expressed as a percentage, it equals 2.1 per cent compared to 3.0 per cent for the period 1995 to 2000. Nevertheless, it is clear that inward FDI to Canada increased relative to the size of the Canadian economy in the second half of the 1990s. A similar pattern is also observed for the United States, and the order of magnitude of the increase is about the same as for Canada. Specifically, in both countries the percentage calculated for the period 1995 to 2000 is about three times the percentage calculated for the period 1990 to 1995.[3] The calculated percentage for Canada then decreases in the 2001 to 2005 period, as is also true for the United States. Indeed, the relative decrease is even more substantial for the United States. Specifically, the calculated percentage for 2001 to 2005 is about half the calculated percentage for 1995 to 2000 in the case of the United States. In the case of Canada, the percentage for the latter period is about two-thirds the value of the percentage calculated for the earlier period.

It is also apparent from Table 10.1 that outward FDI as a percentage of GDP increased in the second half of the 1990s compared to the first half in both the United States and Canada. The increase for Canada was more substantial than in the case of the United States. Moreover, whereas outward FDI as a percentage of GDP declined in the United States during the subperiod 2001 to 2005 compared to the 1995 to 2000 subperiod, the opposite was true for Canada. To be sure, the increase in the calculated percentage for 2001 to 2005 leaves that percentage only slightly higher than the percentage calculated for 1995 to 2000 for Canada.

What is also important to highlight is that outward FDI as a share of GDP has been consistently higher in Canada than in the United States post-1990. This reflects the emergence of major multinational companies in Canada later than occurred in the United States. Consequently, one should be cautious in interpreting the higher share of outward FDI to GDP for Canada post-2001 as indicating that Canadian businesses were investing more in the United States in reaction to post-2001 border security developments. Rather, it is more likely to reflect the continuation of a process whereby relatively young Canadian multinational companies continued to 'build out' their global supply chains at a faster pace than their more mature U.S. counterparts.

Some indirect evidence on the potential motivation for increased outward FDI as a share of GDP for Canada is provided by information contained in Table 10.2. Specifically, Table 10.2 reports the shares of Canadian outward FDI in the United States and elsewhere, where the outward FDI estimates are expressed as stocks – that is, the accumulated value of outward FDI to the date shown. What is noteworthy is the decrease in the relative importance of the United States as a host country for Canadian outward FDI in the post-1990 period. This decrease continued in the post-2001 period, mirroring an increase in the share of Canadian outward FDI going to Europe. While not shown in the table, Canada's share of the U.S. stock of outward FDI was actually higher in 2005 than in 2001 (11.3 per cent compared to 10.4 per cent), although it was lower than the share in 1994 (12.1 per cent). These data suggest that Canada became a relatively more attractive location for U.S. outward FDI in the post-2001 period.

The inference one might draw from Table 10.2, in conjunction with our earlier observation about the increase in Canadian outward FDI as a share of GDP in the post-2001 period, is that the latter increase does not likely reflect 'disinvestment' in Canada on the part of Canadian-based businesses owing, in turn, to border-related security disruptions. Specifically, it seems highly unlikely that Canadian businesses would expand capacity in Europe for purposes of exporting to the United States in order to reduce their reliance on Canada as a location for exporting to the U.S. market. Rather, the expansion of capacity in Europe might well reflect a strategic decision to serve a growing European Union through the activities of European affiliates rather than through exporting.

In summary, a comparison of FDI data for Canada and the United States does not support a conclusion that Canada became a less attractive location for foreign direct investment in the post-9/11 period. An inference one might draw is that the disproportionate disruption to Canadian exports to the United States post-9/11 has not been of a sufficient magnitude to encourage multinational companies to expand production capacity in the United States relative to Canada in order to serve the U.S. domestic market more intensively from facilities within the United States. In this regard, it may be the case that other developments that took place in Canada offset the disadvantage to Canadian exports associated with border disruptions. In particular, improvements in Canadian productivity in the motor vehicles sector relative to the United States may have been a strong offsetting factor favouring continued reinvestment in Canadian motor vehicle assembly and parts facilities. Higher oil, gas, and mineral prices post-2002 may also have contributed to increased FDI into Canada, offsetting any depressing influence of security-related border disruptions.

Other Evidence: Surveys

Some additional evidence on the potential impact of post-9/11 border security developments on the location of production facilities in North America is provided in a previously cited report by MacPherson and McConnell (2005). This report documents the results of a postal survey that was distributed during the late summer of 2004 to executives of business establishments located in southern Ontario and western New York. Several of the survey questions bear on the issue of whether the relative attractiveness of locating in either Canada or the United States was significantly affected by post-9/11 border security developments.

One question asked: 'What is the likelihood that the company will relocate all or some of its production capabilities that are now located in North America, but outside of the home country, back into the home country in order to minimize security-related concerns?' Some 68 per cent of the firms responded that the question was not applicable, which suggests that they did not have North American production facilities located outside of their home country. Another 24 per cent of respondents indicated that they were unlikely or uncertain about such a move. Only 8 per cent of the firms indicated that they were very or somewhat likely to relocate production facilities back to their home base as a result of security-related concerns.

A second question asked: 'What is the likelihood that the company will move some of its domestic operations across the border to the other North American nation in order to minimize security-related matters?' Some 47 per cent of respondents answered that the question was not applicable. Such a response is somewhat puzzling in this context, since the responding firms presumably had domestic operations. The authors of the survey report do not explain the relatively high 'inapplicable' response rate to this question. One possible inference is that the requirement for maintaining domestic operations is so paramount that relocation across the border is ordinarily not even thought of as a viable option. More conclusively, some 43 per cent of respondents indicated that they were unlikely or uncertain about such a transfer. Only 10 per cent of respondents replied that they were very or somewhat likely to transfer operations across the border to the neighbouring country.

In summary, the responses reported to the two questions bearing on the likely relocation of businesses in Ontario and New York State reinforce our earlier conclusion from FDI patterns in North America. Namely, post-9/11 security-related disruptions to bilateral trade flows have not resulted in North American businesses relocating production facilities within North America to any significant extent, or, perhaps, that any incentives to relocate associated with border security procedures have been offset by other factors.

Other Evidence: Production Patterns

Another possible interpretation of the evidence presented to this point is that business relocation decisions are long-term. Hence, while there may be no obvious evidence of geographical relocation of production facilities in the immediate post-9/11 period, one might anticipate significant future relocations if the status quo with respect to trade disruptions persists. In this context, a possible early indication of future reinvestment decisions is whether capacity utilization rates in the same industry differ between Canada and the United States. In particular, one might hypothesize that U.S.-based production establishments increased their capacity utilization in response to the relatively significant border security–related disruptions to Canadian exports to the United States. In a similar manner, Canadian production establishments may have decreased their capacity utilization, as their affiliates in the U.S. undertook more of their own production while acquiring less from the Canadian affiliates.

The motor vehicle industry arguably offers an excellent case study for assessing the degree to which production location decisions were affected by post-9/11 developments. For one thing, the motor vehicle industry is the single largest bilateral trade sector. For another, much of the production capacity of the sector is owned by multinational companies with facilities on both sides of the border. Those companies are, therefore, in a relatively good position to 'reorganize' production activity, since any such reorganization can simply be mandated by management decisions.

Hence, if border disruptions are contributing to a significant competitive disadvantage for Canadian-based producers, one might expect to see the major auto producers shift more production towards their U.S.-based plants relative to their Canadian-based plants in the post-9/11 period. In this regard, Globerman (2004) looked at production activity in North American car and truck assembly plants in the aftermath of 9/11. Specifically, he looked at Canada's share of North American car and truck production for the years 2001 to 2003. For cars, Canada's share was 20.3 per cent in 2001. It then decreased to 18.8 per cent in 2002 but subsequently increased to 19.1 per cent in 2003. For trucks, Canada's share was 12.3 per cent in 2001. It increased to 12.6 per cent in 2002 and then declined to 12.3 per cent in 2003. On the whole, therefore, there was no notable decrease in production activity away from Canada in favour of the United States that might be expected to presage a decrease in capital investment in Canada relative to the United States in North America's largest trade sector.

To be sure, the evidence cited above suggesting that Canada's share of North American car and truck production was relatively stable in the post-9/11 period is based on a short time span; however, more recent data also support this evaluation. Specifically, through October 2005, Canada's share of North American car production for the year was approximately 20 per cent, while its share of truck production for the same time period was around 13.5 per cent.[4] Hence, Canada's share of automobile production through the first ten months of 2005 was very slightly below its share in 2001, while its share of truck production was modestly above its share in 2001. Overall, it seems prudent to conclude that there is no evidence of a significant shift away from Canada as a source of North American motor vehicle production in the post-9/11 period.

With respect to the production of automobiles and parts, it might be noted that the transportation equipment sector has bilateral trade shipments concentrated in a small number of ports. Indeed, the crossing between Detroit and Windsor is the major port for bilateral automobile shipments. It should be recalled that the Canadian export trade shortfall through the Windsor/Detroit crossing had essentially 'disappeared' by 2004. It might, therefore, be the case that auto production in the United States did not increase relative to production in Canada, at least in part, because the multinational automobile companies, as well as local, state, and provincial government officials responded effectively to the border disruptions at the Windsor/Detroit crossing. While a full consideration of this possibility is beyond the scope of this study, the fact that other ports, less intensively involved with automobile shipments, did experience a sustained Canadian export shortfall serves as a caution that the sustained production experience of the Canadian automobile sector might not be characteristic of other Canadian industries.

Investment and Trade

To the extent that Canadian exporters are still experiencing trade shortfalls associated with post-9/11 border security developments, whereas U.S. exporters are apparently not, it is somewhat surprising that Canadian automobile production and inward FDI are not obviously lagging comparable statistics for the United States. One possibility that must be acknowledged is that our failure to hold constant other possible determinants of production and capital investment is obscuring the fact that these other determinants are, on balance, favourable to Canadian industrial expansion and that, in the absence of these other factors, the negative influence of border security developments would be more apparent in the data. A second possibility is that investment relocation decisions take a long time, and, therefore, the negative impacts of export shortfalls on capital investments in Canada, particularly by multinational companies, will become more apparent in the future.

Yet another possibility is that relatively rapid growth of domestic demand in Canada more than compensated for Canada's export shortfall such that there has been little economic pressure to curtail production and capital investment relative to the United States. The data reported in Table 10.3 lend some support to this presumption. Specifically, Table 10.3 reports the annual average percentage growth in real total domestic demand for the two countries for specific years. Real total domestic demand is the inflation-adjusted value of total domestic expenditures in each country. As shown in the table, with the exception of 2004, real total domestic demand grew faster in Canada than in the United States over the post-2001 period.

To this point we have established that domestic demand grew faster in Canada than in the United States in the post-9/11 period, while foreign direct investment patterns do not appear to have shifted away from Canada in favour of the United States. Moreover, at least in the case of the motor vehicle industry, production does not seem to have increased in the United States relative to Canada. All of these observations support an inference that the export shortfall suffered by Canada has not resulted in a significant reduction in capital investment in Canada relative to the United States, subject to the caveat that we have not held constant the determinants of these economic variables in order to identify the unique influence of post-9/11 border security developments.

The final point to consider is whether private-sector capital investment in Canada has declined relative to private-sector capital formation in the United States in the post-2001 period. This variable will encompass investment by all private-sector companies in Canada and not just multinational companies. Since multinational companies may have been able to adjust to border-related disruptions more effectively than smaller domestically owned companies in Canada, it is useful to consider the investment behaviour of the total private sector.

In Table 10.4, annual average percentage growth rates for gross fixed private-sector domestic capital investment are reported for 1999 to 2005 for Canada and the United States.[5] No clear post-9/11 pattern is identifiable in the series. Specifically, domestic capital formation increased in Canada relative to the United States in 2002 and 2003, whereas the opposite was the case in 2004 and 2005. Over the full period 2002 to 2005, the average annual increase in gross fixed domestic investment in Canada (4.8 per cent) exceeded the average annual increase in the United States (4.1 per cent).

Overall Summary and Conclusion

A significant concern on the part of Canadian business leaders and government officials is that the documented post-9/11 border disruptions will put Canadian-based businesses at a competitive disadvantage compared to their U.S.-based counterparts, which over time will lead to a 'migration' of private-sector investment away from Canada in favour of the United States. Our earlier finding of a persisting export shortfall for Canada heightens this concern; however, the evidence reviewed in this chapter suggests that the feared investment displacement is not yet evident, at least in observed patterns of FDI and domestic capital formation.

Since we have not specified and estimated a model of capital investment, we are unable to reject the argument that capital investment rates in Canada would have been even higher in the post-9/11 period were it not for export trade shortfalls associated with border security procedures at major border crossings. Nor can we reject the argument that reactions of investors take time, and that investment rates in Canada will ultimately suffer if the barrier to Canadian exports implicitly posed by border security procedures persists. In this regard, the slower rate of domestic capital investment in Canada compared to the United States in 2004 and 2005 may reflect a longer-run reaction to post-9/11 developments.

Yet another qualification that should be borne in mind is that domestic demand increased at a faster rate in Canada than in the United States over the period 2002 to 2005, and that some of the factors contributing to the growth of domestic demand in Canada might be especially relevant to the period in question, including higher energy prices. It may also be the case that the export shortfall resulted in an increased domestic supply of goods that were otherwise bound for the U.S. market. The resulting lower domestic prices could be expected to contribute to increased domestic sales. The booming energy industry post-2001 may also have contributed to an increase in domestic investment that obscures any depressing effect of export shortfalls on capital investment in Canada's manufacturing industries.

In theory, it seems unlikely that a persisting security-related barrier to Canadian exports to the United States will not ultimately materialize in slower rates of capital investment in Canada than would otherwise be the case. Even if Canadian exporters cultivate larger domestic markets for their products, it seems likely that this would result in lower prices and, probably, lower profit margins for those exporters. Lower profit margins, in turn, will discourage capital investment, at the margin. Since capital investment is an important channel for introducing technological change into the Canadian economy, the persistence of an export shortfall could have potentially broad and adverse consequences for all Canadians.

11 Summary and Policy Conclusions

The main finding of interest in this study is that the disruptive impacts of post-9/11 security developments on Canada–U.S. trade did have a significant and negative impact on the growth of Canada–U.S. trade. While this impact apparently dissipated for U.S. exports to Canada by 2004, they persisted for U.S. imports from Canada, at least through the middle of 2005.

The negative impact on Canadian exports to the United States is of obvious concern to Canadian policy makers, particularly in light of Canada's extreme dependence on the United States as a market for its products; however, the persisting negative impact on U.S. imports from Canada should also be of concern to U.S. policy makers. As noted earlier, U.S. and Canadian producers are increasingly linked through interdependent supply chains such that efficient production in one country depends on the timely arrival of parts, components, and other inputs from the other country. Therefore, disruptions of imports from Canada will oblige U.S. producers to substitute domestic production for imports in order to maintain existing levels of output. Presumably, domestic production is more costly or otherwise less desirable than importing from Canada or the original level of importing would not have occurred in the first place. The end result of a disruption of imports from Canada will therefore be higher costs for U.S. producers that, in turn, may be partly or completely passed through to U.S. consumers in the form of higher prices.

Furthermore, even though it appears that the negative impacts on trade of 9/11-related security developments diminished over time, our findings highlight the dangers posed to bilateral trade by future security breaches. While one fervently hopes that we never again experience the horror of 9/11, it may not take a security breach on such a monumental scale to cause serious disruption of bilateral trade. The point here is that policy makers should not be sanguine about the current state of affairs insofar as border security and trade relations are concerned. Few experts believe that the 'fixes' that have been made, to date, successfully marry security-related concerns with the imperative to reduce the costs and other disadvantages associated with meeting border security-related regulations and procedures. It is, therefore, appropriate to consider this question: Where should we go from here in terms of balancing security and commercial imperatives in the bilateral context?

Policy Options

Andreas (2003) identifies three broad directions in which North American border security policies might go: (1) unilateral fortification and hardening of U.S. border defences, with security trumping all other considerations; (2) multilateral policy harmonization and a pooling of sovereignty to build a formal North American security perimeter; (3) a mixture of enhanced cross-border security coordination and collaboration with partial and uneven policy convergence.

The first option was essentially the U.S. response in the immediate aftermath of 9/11. As Flynn (2003) notes, the virtual closing of the border immediately after 9/11 created quick and severe hardship for U.S. companies, particularly in the automobile sector, and the U.S. government was relatively quick to acknowledge that security concerns must coexist with commercial interests. It might also be argued that U.S. officials recognized the importance of collaboration with their Canadian counterparts to address the disruptive effects on trade of heightened border security. While there are some politicians and commentators in the United States who express the view that U.S. security should not be 'outsourced' to other countries, the reality that most U.S. policy makers recognize is that it would be prohibitively expensive, if not completely impractical, for the United States to assume the unilateral responsibility for screening all commercial shipments entering the United States from foreign countries. Hence, the policy dialogue appropriately is focused on the nature of cooperation between Canada and the United States.

A frequently discussed option for multilateral policy harmonization is the implementation of a border security perimeter in which commercial shipments and travellers entering the North American 'space' would face security screening at the point of entry. Once cleared to enter, they could cross the Canadian–U.S. border presumably without the need for additional security evaluation. A model of a common external perimeter is the European Union's Schengen Agreement. This agreement includes common visa and asylum policies, a shared information system, and standardized border procedures. Adoption of a Schengen-type approach to harmonizing border security seems unlikely for a number of reasons. Perhaps the most prominent reason is that Canadian officials see the harmonization of visa and related immigration policies as meaning that Canada must conform to U.S. policies, and they are reluctant to do so. While Canadian officials might well argue that Canada's visa and immigration policies are preferable to those of the United States on both economic and humanitarian grounds, the ostensible Canadian government objection to a Schengen-type arrangement is the de facto ceding of national sovereignty in matters of great significance to Canadians.

While full harmonization of border management issues along the lines of the European Union seems unlikely for the foreseeable future, bilateral cooperation, with the coordination of border management initiatives, has a long history and seems the most plausible trajectory for future policies to follow. In this regard, Canada has implemented 'unilateral' security-related policies in the past to address U.S. concerns, and it has also initiated cooperative efforts such as the Smart Border Accord. Given the asymmetric importance of an 'open' border to Canada, it seems reasonable to posit that Canada should continue in its efforts to establish an agenda for future coordinated actions on the part of the two countries while taking unilateral actions that are in its own self-interest.

The Way Forward

If a total harmonization of security policies on a bilateral basis is neither practical nor (perhaps) desirable, what specific initiatives might be considered? This question is obviously quite open-ended, since myriad initiatives might be considered ranging from the relatively mundane (e.g., increase personnel staffing at surface border crossings) to the futuristic (e.g., develop and deploy inspection technologies that can efficiently and accurately confirm the content of shipped cargo and the personal identities of the drivers). We are not in a position of knowledge to make recommendations at such detailed levels of specificity. At a more general level, we can endorse the broad recommendations put forward by Flynn (2003). Namely, policy makers should focus on developing the means to validate in advance the overwhelming majority of the people and goods that cross the border as law-abiding and low risk while enhancing the means of federal agents to target and intercept inbound, high-risk people and goods.

It also seems to us that economic incentives should be mobilized to facilitate the investments in the requisite technology to accomplish the efficient screening procedures that Flynn outlines. For example, shippers might be 'risk rated' by governments on the basis of the speed and reliability of the information they provide on cargo and personnel to those responsible for border security. Risk ratings might also be based on the intrinsic terrorism hazards posed by the cargo being shipped, as well as the ports through which goods are shipped. The latter consideration seems particularly relevant in light of our findings that disruption problems differ across ports. Risk ratings might, in turn, be used to assess 'user fees' applied to shippers and, presumably, passed on to final consumers. The fees collected from shippers would be used for public investments in physical infrastructure and technology deployed at the border to ensure secure and expeditious commercial border crossings.

Under current arrangements, companies that comply with security requirements are eligible for expedited border crossing programs such as FAST. Our suggestion is meant to extend the current approach by linking more closely the costs and benefits to shippers of initiatives to mitigate the risks that their shipping activities pose to the public, as well as the costs incurred by governments to address those risks. Individual shippers and shipments are unlikely to be equally risky from a security standpoint. Equivalently, they are unlikely to impose the same costs on authorities charged with enforcing border security. Current programs that oblige companies either to opt in or opt out fundamentally obscure distinctions among companies regarding the value that each places on membership in the program, as well as differences in the costs imposed by individual companies on the 'security maintenance system' by dint of the type of cargo they carry. Moreover, required programs per expedited crossings, such as C-TPAT, that do not explicitly distinguish among companies with regard to differential risks of shipments, impose substantial upfront fixed and sunk costs that are particularly onerous for small companies.[1]

A risk-rated, user-based payment system could also allow for differences across companies in border crossing time patterns (e.g., by day or by hour). To the extent that there is 'peaking' in specific days or times of day, companies that contribute to the peak load problem implicitly impose more security risk, since inspections would necessarily need to be briefer in order to avoid creating longer waiting times. It is economically efficient, as well as fair, to expect those shippers imposing greater security burdens on society to bear a greater share of the costs associated with dealing with the security burdens.

Overall Conclusions

Policy makers must address two interrelated questions in designing responses to perceived border security risks: (1) What share of society's scarce resources should be dedicated to achieving 'acceptable' levels of border security while facilitating international commerce? (2) How would the resources be best utilized? The questions are extremely difficult to answer, given the intrinsically uncertain nature of the likelihood of terrorist acts, as well as their likely consequences. The questions are further complicated by the merging of the goals of controlling illegal immigration and ensuring transportation security, at least in the United States (Block 2006). Hence, as a practical matter, it is virtually impossible to assess whether the U.S. $22.2 billion that President Bush proposed for border and transportation security in fiscal 2007 represents overspending or underspending from the perspective of the social interest.[2]

Since the 'production function' for border security is also unknown, it is impossible to evaluate whether governments are allocating resources efficiently to the production of border security. The budget proposal outlined in the preceding paragraph seeks approximately $459 million in funding for 1,500 new border protection agents and $100 million for cameras, sensors, and other detection equipment to be deployed along both the Canadian and Mexican borders (ibid.). For those who believe that new electronic technologies are the key to efficiently securing our borders, the emphasis in the proposed budget on increasing the number of agents might seem inappropriate. On the other hand, survey evidence suggests that waiting times for commercial shippers crossing the border are most strongly related to the number of lanes open for inspecting, and the latter is a function of staffing levels.

In short, policy prescriptions must be modest, at the present time, to reflect the very limited knowledge we have about the relevant policy environment. While our findings provide only a modest amount of new information to the policy-making process, several implications of our findings are worth highlighting. One implication is that Canada must continue to promote efforts by the U.S. government to ensure that security concerns do not unduly constrain Canada's ability to ship goods to the United States. In this regard, controversial policies in Canada, such as Bill C-11, which is intended to limit access to appeals by rejected refugee claimants and to make it easier to deport individuals whose requests for asylum have been rejected, as well as Bill C-36, which provides for additional resources and police powers to identify and punish terrorists and terrorist support groups, must be seen not just as initiatives to promote domestic security, but also as actions that can help enlist U.S. government interest in keeping the border open to commercial shipments from Canada. It seems likely that the U.S. government will always be willing to err on the side of perceived increased border security at the expense of relatively easy and low-cost transborder shipping conditions, and our results are consistent with a view that Canadian exporters will suffer disproportionate damage from this U.S. preference. As such, and however unpleasant the implication for Canadian nationalists, Canadian security measures must be calibrated against the reactions they will elicit in the United States.

Another implication is that border security policies should acknowledge relevant differences in conditions and circumstances at individual border crossing locations. While our results implicitly identify differences for border crossings on the U.S. side, it would not be surprising if similar differences could be identified for land ports on the Canadian side. Clearly, there are some compelling advantages to standardizing border security procedures across all ports; however, to the extent that causes of shipment disruptions differ across ports, as well as in terms of the riskiness of the commercial shipments passing through individual ports, there is a strong case to be made for allowing individual ports some leeway to differentiate strategies and tactics for safeguarding commercial shipments from terrorist actions while permitting those shipments to flow freely across the border.

Finally, and notwithstanding our earlier scepticism about the practicality and desirability of full integration of border security procedures on a bilateral basis, it is clear that coordination of infrastructure investments by governments on both sides of the border is imperative if infrastructure investments are to be effective. Clearly, capacity expansions on one side of the border may have minimal impacts on the actual speed and consistency of shipping times if bottlenecks on the other side persist. Moreover, there are likely to be significant cost savings by harmonizing the timing of infrastructure investments on each side of the border. On this score, investments being undertaken under the auspices of the Government of Canada's Border Infrastructure Fund seem an appropriate approach, as they involve cooperation on the part of federal, provincial, and local authorities, including operators of bridges and tunnels that provide rights of way to ports on either side of the border.

In addition, more effective integration between agencies of the two countries is needed with respect to the operation of jointly administered security clearance programs and the like. Webber (2005) offers the example of Canadian personnel responsible for administering Canada's counterpart program to the U.S. program for carrier and shipper best practices under the C-TPAT program not knowing which shippers and carriers appearing at Canadian ports and borders are members of C-TPAT. The ostensible reason is U.S. concern over C-TPAT members' statutory rights against disclosure. He also highlights the need for the two governments to implement effective incentives for businesses to invest in and commit themselves to ensuring greater security for shipments. Much as we do, he criticizes 'take it or leave it' programs such as FAST as not providing clear and strong incentives to private companies, at the margin.

Technological change is a source of optimism for public- and private-sector policy makers seeking to improve the speed and ease of commercial shipping while achieving increasingly higher levels of security. Companies are increasingly investing in new technologies to facilitate management of their supply chains. These technologies can and should be married with hardware and software innovations that facilitate identification of the contents of cargo and the identities of carriers. Explicit efforts on the part of business and government to integrate research and development efforts directed at logistics and security could have large social payoffs, not the least of which might be faster growth of bilateral trade.

Notes

1. Introduction

1 A comprehensive discussion of this agreement is contained in Meyers (2003). Earlier negotiations between Canada and the United States facilitated the relatively quick implementation of the U.S.–Canada Smart Border Declaration. For example, the 1997 Border Vision Initiative focused on improving information sharing and interagency coordination. On this latter point, see Belelieu (2003).

2 Throughout this report, we will refer to specific land border crossings using the official names as provided by each country's border agency. The exception is in our statistical analysis in later chapters. There we employ data collected at the U.S. port-of-entry level. Hence, when discussing our empirical analysis, our port references pertain to U.S. ports of entry. Chapter 2 discusses in some detail the geographical links between our sample of U.S. ports and their paired Canadian crossings.

3 See Lee, Martin, Ouellet, and Vaillancourt (2005). Exporters that do nothing to adjust to the demands of U.S. security programs such as C-TPAT can still bring their products to the U.S. market.

4 During the busiest periods, there may be six to eight booths open. See Battelle (2003).

5 Details and evaluations of the U.S. and Canadian reorganizations of border management procedures are provided in Meyers (2005).

6 To be sure, other attributes of the border environment are implicated besides security concerns. For example, Meyers (2005) concludes that predictable border crossing times remains an elusive goal, in part because of inadequate physical infrastructure at border crossings.

7 For example, the Coalition (2005, 2) argues that after the Smart Border Declaration of 2001, processing times for shipments entering the U.S.

increased from 45 seconds to over 2 minutes and 15 seconds per truck by the end of 2004.

8 Whether border security and expedited cross-border commerce represent conflicting objectives is discussed in Flynn (2003).

9 The concept of risk management in the context of Canada–U.S. border security arrangements is discussed in Chapter 2.

10 To be sure, governments might impose 'user fees' or other usage-related schemes to defray some or all of the additional expenditures. However, since maintenance of the international border and conditions of entry is a government responsibility, any significant changes in security and security-related procedures are intrinsically public activities.

11 Again, we note that U.S. export data at the individual port level are available only beginning in 1997.

12 Note that our analysis of trade flows pre- and post-9/11 uses data referencing exports and imports through U.S. land ports. This approach reflects the fact that detailed commodity trade flows at the port level are available from U.S. data sources (as described in a later chapter). Moreover, there has been more concern about shipment delays for goods crossing into the United States from Canada than for the reverse flow.

2. Security Policy and the Canada–U.S. Border

1 www.internationalboundarycommission.org.

2 These offices are listed on the CBSA website at www.cbsa.gc.ca/contact/listing/indexpages/indextype15-e.html.

3 The map is based on information obtained from the website of Glover Customs Brokers of Ottawa, Ontario.

4 These provincial maps were taken from the CBSA website and are reproduced by permission.

5 The Canadian crossing located at Four Falls, New Brunswick, does not have a corresponding U.S. office and so does not provide access to the United States.

6 Lists of U.S. ports of entry for each state are available from the Customs and Border Protection website: www.cbp.gov/xp/cgov/toolbox/ports.

7 www.cbp.gov/xp/cgov/border_security.

3. Overview of Canada–U.S. Trade in Goods

1 As explained in chapter 2, there are some seventy-five U.S. land ports-of-entry along the Canada–U.S border.

2 Over 60 per cent of Canadian exports to the United States originate in Ontario (Goldfarb and Robson 2003).

3 In this regard, the port of Buffalo processed the largest share of personal vehicle crossings from Canada (around 23 per cent in 2002), followed by Detroit (21 per cent) and Port Huron (7 per cent).

4 The remainder of exports and imports are accounted for by the residual modes: mail and 'other.'

4. The Impacts of Border Security – Review of the Literature

1 We are aware of preliminary research by the Conference Board of Canada that relies on similar statistical approaches to those we adopt in this study.

2 While the latter are tied to higher fuel prices in recent years, increased waiting times and higher associated fuel costs for shippers undoubtedly strengthened the incentives of shippers to add fuel surcharges.

3 Authors' interview with James Pettinger, 14 July 2005.

4 The survey is discussed in a Canada NewsWire story titled 'Cross-Border Delays Too Long: Canadian Carriers' (www.newswire.ca/en/releases/archive/August2002/21/c4317.html).

5 Bonsor (2004, 15), among others, highlights the fact that not all of the major border-crossing points have dedicated FAST lanes, so FAST-certified shipments must sit in line with non-FAST traffic.

6 Lee and her colleagues (2005) report that carriers crossing the border from Quebec spend from two minutes to several hours actually clearing U.S. Customs, although the delays are not entirely attributable to security-related procedures.

7 The Coalition for Secure and Trade-Efficient Borders (2005, 2) asserts that North American businesses face 'billions of dollars of compliance and delay costs at the border.'

8 These authors also note that waiting times and, perhaps, variability of waiting times were already increasing prior to 9/11 owing to increased congestion. This point is also made in a report of the Ontario Chamber of Commerce (2004).

9 See, for example, Ontario Chamber of Commerce (2004).

10 Globerman (2005) uses data through the third quarter of 2003 to extrapolate a further decline in the ratio of Canadian exports to U.S. GDP in that year.

11 On the other hand, transportation equipment, which Goldfarb and Robson rated as relatively vulnerable to border disruptions, was the worst subindex in terms of stock market performance, whereas oil producers, rated as relatively invulnerable, performed best.

12 Goldfarb and Robson also examine changes in employment for Canadian industries classified as more or less vulnerable to border disruptions. They find only a slight tendency for industries rated as more vulnerable to show worse employment numbers.

13 Conversely, Bonsor (2004) highlights the problems in the cross-border rail market that arise when U.S. Customs and Immigration wants to do a physical search of a train, particularly when it wants to physically examine a container on a train. While only around 2 per cent of containers are subject to a physical examination, delays can amount to hours when inspections do occur.

14 For a different time period, Battelle (2003) reports that there was some very modest switching between the two main Michigan ports by truckers in the post-9/11 period.

5. Study Methodology

1 Data were available for U.S. imports from Canada beginning in 1996. For U.S. exports to Canada, data were available only starting in 1997.

2 Frankel and Rose (2002) state that the gravity framework is one of the more successful empirical models in economics.

3 Obviously, average distances travelled for Canadian exports to the U.S. or for U.S. exports to Canada might vary over time if the mix of either country's exports changes over time; however, in the absence of major shifts of production and consumption locales, border distances applicable to any specific export should be constant over time.

4 For example, both countries deregulated a number of major industries in the post-1960 period, although the United States deregulated sooner in most cases than did Canada.

5 More technically, the influence of time invariant factors will be captured by the estimated constant term, that is, B_0 in our equation (page 46).

6 One might therefore include a simple binomial variable that takes a value of zero prior to 9/11 and a value of one after 9/11.

7 Other developments might also be relevant, although the two mentioned above seem to us to be of greatest potential relevance.

8 We estimated trade equations at the individual commodity level. Unfortunately, the statistical results were both unstable and unreliable. Hence, they are not reported in this study.

9 The shorter time period for U.S. exports is a consequence of the unavailability of Census export data for periods prior to 1997.

10 Two criteria are of primary relevance in evaluating the statistical reliability of our trade equations. One is the overall goodness of fit of the equa-

tions. The second is the consistency of the signs of the regression coefficients with theoretical expectations.

6. The Aggregate Export and Import Equations

1 This variable is expressed as a seasonally adjusted annual rate. All variables are summarized in Table 6.1.
2 The exchange rate is an average of the daily values for each quarter.
3 The coefficient for each individual land port can be interpreted as the difference between total imports entering that specific port and imports entering through the residual category of ports, holding other variables constant. The positive value of the coefficient for Detroit shows that imports entering through Detroit exceed imports entering through the residual category. Coefficients for the port dummies are reported only for Model 1, as they are virtually unchanged across the various models.
4 Data for U.S. exports for 1996 were unavailable from the Census Bureau.
5 In particular, only the port of Detroit has a positive coefficient.
6 Each estimated coefficient for the individual time dummy variables is the derivative of the dependent variable (ln exports) with respect to time, where the time variable equals unity. Hence, the estimated coefficient is the differential of ln exports, which is simply the relative change in exports.
7 The equations for the exchange rate lagged five and six quarters produced unlikely coefficient estimates for the GDP variable and are therefore not reported.
8 It is worth noting that 95 per cent confidence intervals around the small positive and negative numbers for 2004 and 2005 would include zero.

7. Estimating Export and Import Equations at the Port Level

1 It should be noted that we do not test whether the estimated coefficients between any paired time periods are significantly different from zero. It should also be noted that the estimated coefficient for the 2005 time dummy variable is statistically insignificant in the case of Highgate Springs.
2 It might be noted that the estimated coefficient for the 2005 time dummy for Sweetgrass is statistically insignificant at the .05 level.

8. Interpreting the Estimated Impacts on Overall Bilateral Trade

1 Note that any potentially relevant excluded variables cannot include the

traditional trade determinants that are explicitly included in our model.

2 Hufbauer and Schott (2005) point out that in the post-NAFTA period, transplants accounted for a larger portion of the market share lost by the Big Three than did imports.

3 Conversely, intraindustry trade between the United States and Mexico decreased more dramatically over that period.

4 This simply means that the increases in barrels of oil or in cubic metres of natural gas will be proportionally less than the decreases in the prices of oil and natural gas.

5 Given the geographically integrated North American market for natural gas, U.S. export prices to Canada were quite close to U.S. import prices for natural gas imported from Canada.

6 The basic notion here is that increases in underlying raw material prices will largely be mirrored in changes in prices for fabricated products using those materials.

7 A short history of the U.S.–Canada softwood lumber dispute is found in Random Lengths (2005).

8 The adverse impact of lower commodity prices on exports would be experienced particularly by Canada. At the same time, the 2000–1 recession, in combination with the collapse of the NASDAQ stock market, led to substantial reductions in purchases of telecommunications and computer equipment, which presumably reduced exports of these products by both countries.

9. Interpreting the Estimated Impacts at Individual Ports

1 Highgate Springs is the exception; there, electrical machinery is the single largest import category.

2 To be sure, complaints and concerns have been expressed about transportation bottlenecks surrounding major surface ports on both sides of the border that pre-date 9/11.

3 It should be noted, however, that the longest border crossing delays prior to 9/11 were reported for southbound freight crossing the Blue Water Bridge, that is, for Canadian exports to the United States crossing through Port Huron. See Bonsor (2004, 10).

4 Bonsor (2004, 14) states that around 2 per cent of containers are subject to physical inspection according to available information. He also highlights the fact that Canada Customs has a formal agreement with railways to inspect trains at the first available yard or terminal, unlike the U.S. procedure, which is to inspect at the border as opposed to a yard or terminal. The consequence is that the inspection of individual trains by Canada

Customs doesn't necessarily contribute to a backlog of trains waiting to cross.

5 See Infrastructure Canada, 'Canada-Ontario Announce $325 Million for Border Improvements,' news release, 21 May 2003.

6 Trucks and drivers, on the other hand, do not represent sunk cost investments.

10. Potential Impacts on Capital Investment

1 Some examples of statistical FDI equations for Canada can be found in Kudrle (1995), Globerman and Shapiro (1999), and Hejazi and Safarian (1999). A discussion of FDI modelling more generally is found in Globerman and Shapiro (2002). Time dummy variables similar to those used in our trade equations would presumably be included in the equations to capture the influence of post-9/11 developments.

2 For an extended discussion of the determinants of agglomeration economies, see Krugman (1991) and Rosenthal and Strange (2003).

3 Also similar to the case of Canada, the ratio of inward FDI to GDP in 1995–9 is significantly below the ratio calculated for 1995–2000.

4 See the Auto Channel (2005).

5 It should be cautioned that capital investment changes can be quite volatile in the short run.

11. Summary and Policy Conclusions

1 Lee and her colleagues (2005) conclude that the cost of C-TPAT compliance as a percentage of the value of exports for Quebec-based companies is 17 for small companies in their sample but declines to less than 1 for medium and large companies.

2 The $22.2 billion represents about 35 per cent of the total $58.2 billion proposed for homeland security spending by government (Block 2006).

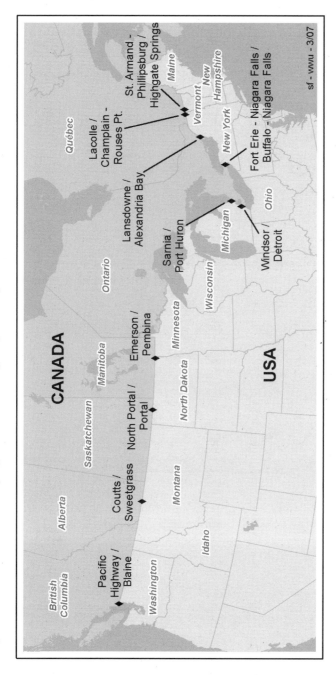

Map 2.1. The Canada–U.S. border region with main highway crossings

Source: Glover Trade, reproduced by permission

Map 2.2a. Canadian highway–land border offices: Yukon

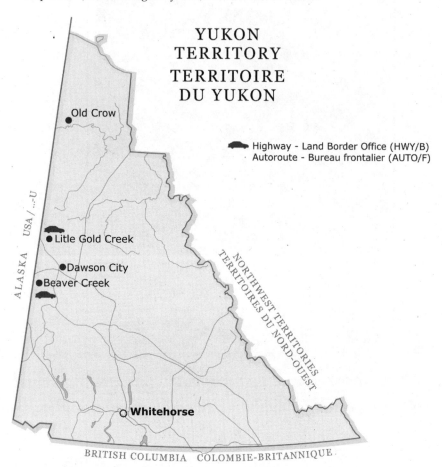

Source: Canada Border Services Agency. Reproduced with permission of the Minister of Public Works and Government Services Canada, 2007.

Map 2.2b. Canadian highway–land border offices: British Columbia

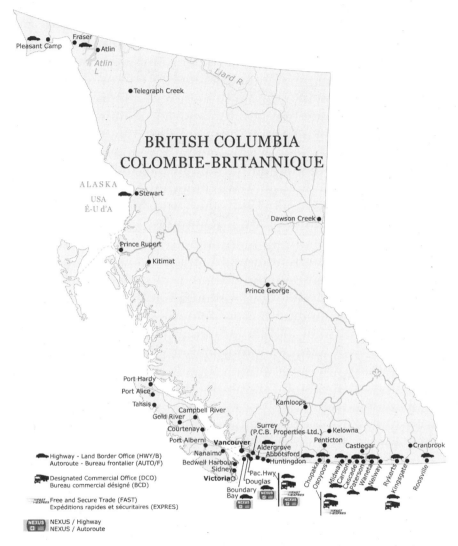

Source: Canada Border Services Agency. Reproduced with permission of the Minister of Public Works and Government Services Canada, 2007.

Map 2.2c. Canadian highway–land border offices: Alberta

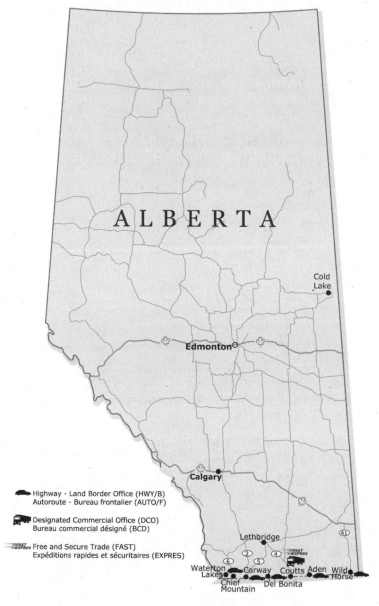

Source: Canada Border Services Agency. Reproduced with permission of the Minister of Public Works and Government Services Canada, 2007.

Map 2.2d. Canadian highway–land border offices: Saskatchewan

Source: Canada Border Services Agency. Reproduced with permission of the Minister of Public Works and Government Services Canada, 2007.

Map 2.2e. Canadian highway–land border offices: Manitoba

Source: Canada Border Services Agency. Reproduced with permission of
the Minister of Public Works and Government Services Canada, 2007.

Map 2.2f. Canadian highway–land border offices: Northern Ontario

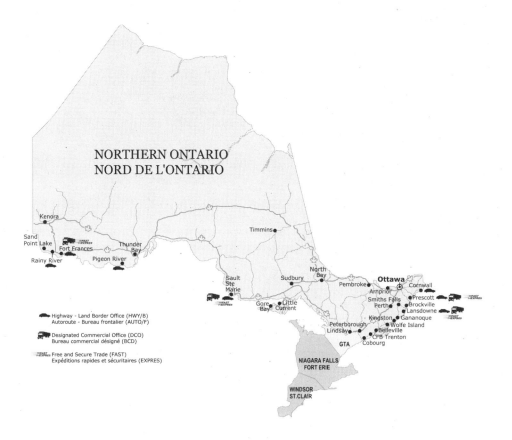

Source: Canada Border Services Agency. Reproduced with permission of the Minister of Public Works and Government Services Canada, 2007.

Map 2.2g. Canadian highway–land border offices: Windsor Region

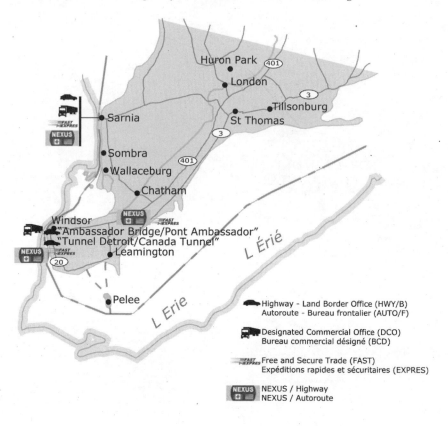

Source: Canada Border Services Agency. Reproduced with permission of the Minister of Public Works and Government Services Canada, 2007.

Map 2.2h. Canadian highway–land border offices: Niagara Region

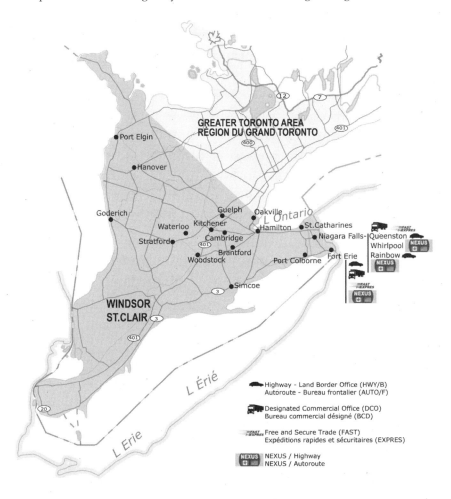

Source: Canada Border Services Agency. Reproduced with permission of the Minister of Public Works and Government Services Canada, 2007.

Map 2.2i. Canadian highway–land border offices: Quebec

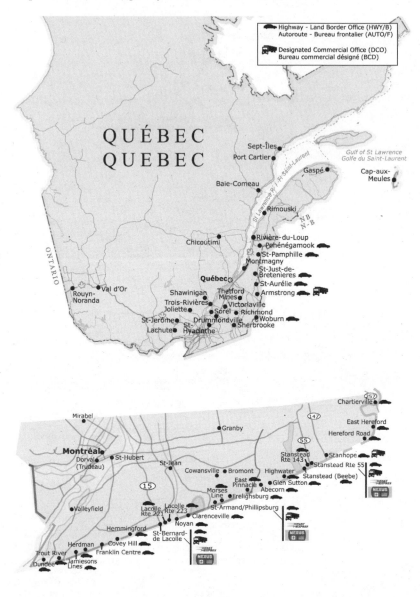

Source: Canada Border Services Agency. Reproduced with permission of the Minister of Public Works and Government Services Canada, 2007.

Map 2.2j. Canadian highway–land border offices: New Brunswick

Source: Canada Border Services Agency. Reproduced with permission of the Minister of Public Works and Government Services Canada, 2007.

Tables and Figures

Tables

Figures

Table 2.1a. U.S. and Canadian border crossings: Maine

U.S. crossing	Port of entry	Port ID	Canadian crossing	Province	Office #
Lubec	Lubec	103	Campobello	NB	225
Jackman	Jackman	104	Armstrong	QC	329
St Aurelie	Jackman	104	Ste-Aurélie	QC	339
St-Just-De-Bretenieres	Jackman	104	St-Just-De-Bretenieres	QC	336
St Pamphile	Jackman	104	St-Pamphile	QC	335
Coburn Gore	Jackman	104	Woburn	QC	208
Vanceboro	Vanceboro	105	St. Croix	NB	205
Monticello	Houlton	106	Bloomfield	NB	212.1
Forest City	Houlton	106	Forest City	NB	212.2
Orient	Houlton	106	Fosterville	NB	212.3
Houlton	Houlton	106	Woodstock Road	NB	212
Fort Fairfield	Fort Fairfield	107	Andover	NB	214
Easton	Fort Fairfield	107	River De Chute	NB	215.1
Hamlin	Van Buren	108	Grand Falls	NB	217
Van Buren	Van Buren	108	St Leonard	NB	218
Madawaska	Madawaska	109	Edmundston	NB	213
Fort Kent	Fort Kent	110	Clair	NB	216
Estcourt Station	Fort Kent	110	Pohenegamook	QC	331
Milltown	Calais	115	Milltown	NB	211.1
Calais	Calais	115	St. Stephen	NB	211
Limestone	Limestone	118	Gillespie Portage	NB	219
Bridgewater	Bridgewater	127	Centreville	NB	215

Table 2.1b. U.S. and Canadian border crossings: Vermont and New Hampshire

U.S. crossing	Port of entry	Port ID	Canadian crossing	Province	Office #
Bridgewater	Bridgewater	127	Centreville	NB	215
Richford	Richford	203	Abercorn	QC	318
Pinnacle	Richford	203	East Pinnacle	QC	369
West Berkshire	Richford	203	Frelighsburg	QC	332
East Richford	Richford	203	Glen Sutton	QC	370
Beecher Falls	Beecher Falls	206	East Hereford	QC	362
North Troy	Derby Line	209	Highwater	QC	334
Derby Line	Derby Line	209	Stanstead (55)	QC	314
Beebe Plain	Derby Line	209	Stanstead (Beebe)	QC	376
Derby Line	Derby Line	209	Stanstead (Rte 143)	QC	375
Pittsburg (NH)	Norton	211	Chartierville	QC	365
Canaan	Norton	211	Hereford Road	QC	366
Norton	Norton	211	Stanhope	QC	354
Alburg Springs	Highgate Springs	212	Clarenceville	QC	337
Morses Line	Highgate Springs	212	Morses Line	QC	367
Alburg Springs	Highgate Springs	212	Noyan	QC	368
Highgate Springs	Highgate Springs	212	St Armand-Philipsburg	QC	328

Table 2.1c. U.S. and Canadian border crossings: New York

U.S. crossing	Port of entry	Port ID	Canadian crossing	Province	Office #
Ogdensburg Bridge	Ogdensburg Bridge	701	Prescott	ON	439
Massena	Massena	704	Cornwall Traffic Office	ON	409
Massena	Massena	704	Dundee	QC	330
Alexandria Bay	Alexandria Bay	708	Lansdowne (Thousand Islands Bridge)	ON	456
Chateauguay	Chateauguay	711	Herdman	QC	307.2
Cannon's Corner	Champlain–Rouses Pt	712	Covey Hill	QC	333.1
Mooers	Champlain–Rouses Pt	712	Hemmingford	QC	333
Champlain	Champlain–Rouses Pt	712	Lacolle: Highway 221	QC	351.1
Rouses Pt	Champlain–Rouses Pt	712	Lacolle: Highway 223	QC	352.2
Champlain	Champlain–Rouses Pt	712	St-Bernard-De-Lacolle: Highway 15	QC	351
Churubusco	Trout River	715	Franklin Centre	QC	307.1
Jamieson Line	Trout River	715	Jamieson's Line	QC	307.3
Malone	Trout River	715	Trout River	QC	307
Buffalo	Buffalo–Niagara Falls	901	Fort Erie (Peace Bridge)	ON	410
Niagara Falls	Buffalo–Niagara Falls	901	Niagara Falls Rainbow Bridge Operations	ON	427.1
Niagara Falls	Buffalo–Niagara Falls	901	Niagara Falls Whirlpool Bridge Operations	ON	427.2
Lewiston	Buffalo–Niagara Falls	901	Queenston Lewiston Bridge	ON	427

Table 2.1d. U.S. and Canadian border crossings: Washington

U.S. crossing	Port of entry	Port ID	Canadian crossing	Province	Office #
Blaine	Blaine	3004	Douglas	BC	840
Blaine	Blaine	3004	Pacific Highway	BC	813
Sumas	Sumas	3009	Huntingdon	BC	817
Nighthawk	Nighthawk	3011	Chopaka	BC	836
Danville	Danville	3012	Carson	BC	834
Ferry	Ferry	3013	Midway	BC	835
Boundary	Boundary	3015	Waneta	BC	833
Laurier	Laurier	3016	Cascade	BC	816
Point Roberts	Point Roberts	3017	Boundary Bay	BC	815
Oroville	Oroville	3019	Osoyoos	BC	819
Frontier	Frontier	3020	Paterson	BC	832
Lynden	Lynden	3023	Aldergrove	BC	841
Metaline Falls	Metaline Falls	3025	Nelway	BC	828

Table 2.1e. U.S. and Canadian border crossings: Montana and Idaho

U.S. crossing	Port of entry	Port ID	Canadian crossing	Province	Office #
Raymond	Raymond, MT	3301	Regway	SK	607
Eastport	Eastport, ID	3302	Kingsgate	BC	818
Turner	Turner, MT	3306	Climax	SK	619
Porthill	Porthill, ID	3308	Rykerts	BC	822
Scobey	Scobey, MT	3309	Coronach	SK	615
Sweetgrass	Sweetgrass, MT	3310	Coutts	AL	705
Willow Creek	Sweetgrass, MT	3310	Willow Creek	SK	621
Whitetail	Whitetail, MT	3312	Big Beaver	SK	614
Piegan	Piegan, MT	3316	Carway	AL	707
Chief Mountain	Piegan, MT	3316	Chief Mountain	AL	709
Ophiem	Ophiem, MT	3317	West Poplar River	SK	618
Roosville	Roosville, MT	3318	Roosville	BC	824
Morgan	Morgan, MT	3319	Monchy	SK	620
Whitlash	Whitlash, MT	3321	Aden	AL	706
Del Bonita	Del Bonita, MT	3322	Del Bonita	AL	708
Wild Horse	Wild Horse, MT	3323	Wild Horse	AL	711

Table 2.1f. U.S. and Canadian border crossings: North Dakota and Minnesota

U.S. crossing	Port of entry	Port ID	Canadian crossing	Province	Office #
Pembina	Pembina, ND	3401	Emerson	MB	502
Portal	Portal, ND	3403	North Portal	SK	602
Neche	Neche, ND	3404	Gretna	MB	503
St John	St John, ND	3405	Lena	MB	522
Northgate	Northgate, ND	3406	Northgate	SK	613
Walhalla	Walhalla, ND	3407	Winkler	MB	502
Hannah	Hannah, ND	3408	Snowflake	MB	509
Sarles	Sarles, ND	3409	Crystal City	MB	520
Ambrose	Ambrose, ND	3410	Torquay	SK	617
Antler	Antler, ND	3413	Lyleton	MB	523
Sherwood	Sherwood, ND	3414	Carievale	SK	612
Hansboro	Hansboro, ND	3415	Cartwright	MB	521
Maida	Maida, ND	3416	Windygates	MB	519
Fortuna	Fortuna, ND	3417	Oungre	SK	616
Westhope	Westhope, ND	3419	Coulter	MB	524
Noonan	Noonan, ND	3420	Estevan Highway	SK	610
Carbury	Carbury, ND	3421	Goodlands	MB	508
Dunseith	Dunseith, ND	3422	Boissevain	MB	507
Warroad	Warroad, MN	3423	Sprague	MB	505
Baudette	Baudette, MN	3424	Rainy River	ON	488
Pinecreek	Pinecreek, ND	3425	Piney	MB	517
Roseau	Roseau, MN	3426	South Junction	MB	506
Lancaster	Lancaster, MN	3430	Tolstoi	MB	506
International Falls	International Falls, MN	3604	Fort Frances Bridge	ON	478
Grand Portage	Grand Portage, MN	3613	Pigeon River	ON	475

Table 2.1g. U.S. and Canadian border crossings: Michigan

U.S. crossing	Port of entry	Port ID	Canadian crossing	Province	Office #
Detroit	Detroit	3801	Windsor/Ambassador Bridge	ON	453
Detroit	Detroit	3801	Windsor/Detroit And Canada Tunnel	ON	452
Port Huron	Port Huron	3802	Sarnia	ON	440
Sault Ste Marie	Sault Ste Marie	3803	Sault Ste Marie Bridge	ON	441

Table 2.2. Distribution of highway–land border offices by province/territory and level of commercial service

Province/ territory	7 days 24 hours	7 days < 24 hours	5 days < 24 hours	No service
Alberta	1	1	4	0
B.C.	3	2	10	2
Manitoba	1	1	14	0
New Brunswick	2	2	11	2
Ontario	10	0	2	2
Quebec	5	0	24	3
Saskatchewan	1	0	12	0
Yukon	0	2	1	1
	23	8	78	10

Figure 3.1. Distribution of U.S. exports and imports by region (2005)

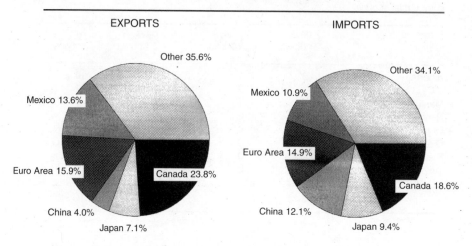

Source: Economic Report of the President, 2005.

Table 3.1. Canada–U.S. trade in goods (millions of USD)

Year	U.S. exports* to Canada	U.S. imports* from Canada
1998	156,734	125,842
1999	166,713	201,287
2000	178,877	233,676
2001	163,259	218,726
2002	160,916	211,756
2003	169,929	224,249
2004	189,982	259,034
2005**	105,492	139,402

Note:
*Current dollars on a balance of payments basis
**First two quarters of 2005, seasonally unadjusted
Source: Department of Commerce, Bureau of Economic Analysis,
www.bea.gov/bea/international/bp_web/simple.cfm?anon=718table_id=108area_id=9

Table 3.2. Leading U.S. imports from Canada (2004 – millions of current USD)

Industry – NAICS		Imports
33611	Autos and motor vehicles	43,171
21111	Oil and gas	40,101
32411	Petroleum products	8,697
32212	Paper products	7,829
32111	Sawmills and wood preservation	7,700
33641	Aerospace products and parts	6,175
32121	Veneer, plywood, and engineered wood products	5,217
33131	Aluminum products	5,166
32521	Resin and synthetic rubber	4,263
33631	Motor vehicle engines and parts	3,997
32619	Other plastic products	3,915
33612	Heavy-duty trucks	2,983
33141	Non-ferrous metals	2,835
33111	Iron and steel	2,712
33637	Motor vehicle metal stamping	2,671
	All Industries	267,478

Source: Government of Canada, Statistics Canada,
strategis.ic.gc.ca/sc_mrkti/tdst/tdo/tdo.php#tag

Table 3.3. Leading U.S. exports to Canada (2004 – millions of current USD)

Industry – NAICS		Exports
33611	Autos and motor vehicles	14,666
33639	Other motor vehicle parts	8,363
33631	Motor vehicle engines and parts	5,767
33635	Motor vehicle transmissions	4,805
32521	Resin and synthetic rubber	4,051
33451	Measuring, medical, and control Instruments	3,876
33411	Computers and peripheral equipment	3,657
33641	Aerospace products and parts	3,362
32541	Pharmaceutical products	3,221
33612	Heavy-duty trucks	3,117
33361	Power transmission equipment	2,734
33111	Iron and steel	2,566
32519	Organic chemicals	2,510
33441	Semiconductors	2,493
21111	Oil and gas	2,423
	All industries	160,549

Source: Government of Canada, Statistics Canada,
strategis.ic.gc.ca/sc_mrkti/tdst/tdo/tdo.php#ta g

Table 3.4. Industrial distribution of U.S. imports from Canada (percentage of total)

	Industry – NAICS	1998	2004
33611	Autos and motor vehicles	18.3	16.1
21111	Oil and gas	6.6	15.0
32212	Paper products	3.9	2.9
32111	Sawmills and wood preservation	3.7	2.9
33641	Aerospace products and parts	2.3	2.3
33411	Computers and peripheral equipment	2.3	0.9
33131	Aluminum products	1.9	1.9
33612	Heavy-duty trucks	1.8	1.1
33441	Semiconductors	1.8	0.8
33631	Motor vehicle engines and parts	1.7	1.5

Source: Government of Canada, Statistics Canada,
strategis.ic.gc.ca/sc_mrkti/tdst/tdo/tdo.php#tag

Table 3.5. Industrial distribution of U.S. exports to Canada (percentage of total)

	Industry – NAICS	1998	2004
33611	Autos and motor vehicles	8.0	9.7
33639	Other motor vehicle parts	5.1	5.2
33631	Motor vehicle engines and parts	3.9	3.6
33411	Computers and peripheral equipment	3.3	2.3
33441	Semiconductors	3.3	1.6
33635	Motor vehicle transmissions	3.1	3.0
33451	Measuring, medical, and control Instruments	2.4	2.4
33641	Aerospace products and parts	2.3	2.1
32521	Resin and synthetic rubber	2.0	2.5
33361	Power transmission equipment	2.0	1.1

Source: Government of Canada, Statistics Canada,
strategis.ic.gc.ca/sc_mrkti/tdst/tdo/tdo.php#tag

Table 3.6. The ten largest U.S. ports at the northern border (2003)
(value of shipment – billions USD)

Port	Exports	Imports
Detroit, MI	55	47
Port Huron, MI	23	40
Buffalo–Niagara Falls, NY	27	32
Champlain–Rouses Point, NY	5	9
Blaine, WA	5	7
Alexandria Bay, NY	4	6
Pembina, ND	5	4
Sweetgrass, MT	4	4
Portal, ND	3	3
Highgate Springs, VT	2	3

Source: U.S. Government, Bureau of Transportation Statistics,
www.bts.gov/publications/americas_freight_transportation_gateways
/introduction_and_overview/html/table_oa.html

Table 4.1. Inbound and outbound waiting times at U.S. border crossings (minutes)

Crossing	Baseline time	Average time	95th percentile time
Detroit outbound	5.7	8.8	13.7
Detroit inbound	12.9	20.4	33.9
Blaine outbound	4.8	21.5	35.3
Blaine inbound	8.1	17.3	35.6
Port Huron outbound	5.0	6.2	9.1
Port Huron inbound	11.1	34.2	80.3
Buffalo outbound	9.0	21.7	38.0
Buffalo inbound	8.3	23.3	83.4

Source: U.S. Department of Transportation, 'Commercial Vehicle Travel Time and Delay at U.S. Border Crossings,' Washington, D.C.: Office of Freight Management and Operations, June 2002

Table 4.2. Border wait times on 12 December 2005

Port crossing	Commercial vehicles wait time	Alternative inspection wait time
Alexandria Bay	65 minutes (5pm EST)	No alternative inspection traffic
Blaine	15 minutes (2pm PST)	No delay (2pm PST)
Buffalo/Niagara Falls (Lewiston Bridge)	No delay (5pm EST)	No alternative inspection traffic
Buffalo/Niagara Falls (Peace Bridge)	5 minutes (5pm EST)	No delay (5pm EST)
Champlain	10 minutes (6pm EST)	No delay (6pm EST)
Detroit (Ambassador Bridge)	No delay (5pm EST)	No delay (5pm EST)
Detroit (Windsor Tunnel)	5 minutes (5pm EST)	5 minutes (5pm EST)
Highgate Springs	8 minutes (3pm EST)	No alternative inspection traffic
Pembina	100 minutes (5pm CST)	No alternative inspection traffic
Port Huron (Bluewater Bridge)	45 minutes (5pm EST)	No delay (5pm EST)
Sweetgrass	10 minutes (3pm MST)	No alternative inspection traffic

Source: U.S. Department of Homeland Security, U.S. Customs and Border Protection, apps.cbp.gov/bwt

Table 6.1. Summary of variables (1996Q1 – 2005Q2, except exports begin in 1997Q1)

	Mean	Maximum	Minimum	Std. Dev.
Exchange rate (Canadian cents per USD)	143.58	159.46	122.08	10.30
Canadian GDP (billions of USD)	$749	$1,095	$599	$146
U.S. GDP (billions of USD)	$9,832	$12,376	$7,624	$1,336
U.S. exports to Canada (millions of USD)	$151,592	$200,828	$125,132	$16,827
U.S. imports from Canada (millions of USD)	$192,116	$259,800	$139,684	$32,270

Sources: Statistics Canada for the exchange rate and Canadian GDP, Bureau of Economic Analysis for U.S. GDP, U.S. Census for the export and import data

Table 6.2. U.S. imports from Canada, 1996Q1 – 2001Q2 models*

Variables	Model 1	Model 2	Model 3	Model 4	Model 5	Model 6	Model 7
Constant	5.64	6.14	7.24	8.60	9.55	10.50	10.96
	(5.55)	(5.98)	(7.01)	(8.74)	(10.58)	(11.93)	(12.24)
GDP	2.04	1.93	1.76	1.56	1.41	1.26	1.20
	(14.65)	(13.91)	(12.65)	(11.78)	(11.69)	(10.72)	(4.26)
Exchange	-.006	-.005	-.003	.001	.004	.007	.008
rate	(-3.35)	(-2.68)	(-1.29)	(0.45)	(2.06)	(3.70)	(4.26)
Q2	.023	.019	.024	.023	.026	.024	.026
	(1.32)	(1.08)	(1.36)	(1.28)	(1.48)	(1.38)	(1.53)
Q3	-.018	-.028	-.023	-.021	-.021	-.015	-.022
	(-1.00)	(-1.52)	(-1.25)	(-1.16)	(-1.14)	(-0.85)	(-1.23)
Q4	.005	-.003	-.004	-.001	-.001	-.001	.009
	(0.29)	(-0.16)	(-0.19)	(-0.04)	(-.01)	(-0.01)	(0.49)
P0212	-2.06						
	(-69.67)						
P0708	-1.84						
	(-62.10)						
P0712	-1.37						
	(-46.36)						
P0901	-.143						
	(-4.84)						
P3004	-1.84						
	(-62.29)						
P3310	-2.39						
	(-80.61)						
P3401	-2.25						
	(-76.10)						
P3403	-2.41						
	(-81.50)						
P3801	.159						
	(5.39)						
P3802	-.179						
	(-6.05)						

$R^2 = .991$ $R^2 = .991$ $R^2 = .991$ $R^2 = .991$ $R^2 = .991$ $R^2 = .991$ $R^2 = .991$

$F_{(15,226)}$ $F_{(15,226)}$

= 1696   = 1666   F = 1627   F = 1617   F = 1646   F = 1714   F = 1746

*a t-statistic is reported below each coefficient

Table 6.3. U.S. exports to Canada, 1997Q1 – 2001Q2

Variables	Model 1	Model 2	Model 3	Model 4	Model 5	Model 6	Model 7
Constant	15.01	14.77	15.21	15.94	17.18	18.86	21.45
	(10.32)	(10.30)	(10.5)	(10.74)	(10.79)	(10.45)	(9.50)
GDP	.881	.908	.848	.731	.520	.214	-.260
	(3.70)	(4.21)	(3.57)	(2.91)	(1.85)	(0.65)	(-0.61)
Exchange	.011	.011	.011	.011	.012	.014	.018
rate	(3.66)	(4.21)	(4.02)	(3.92)	(3.89)	(3.96)	˙(3.96)
Q2	.028	.041	.025	.022	.038	.052	-.015
	(0.73)	(1.06)	(0.65)	(0.56)	(0.92)	(1.33)	(-0.35)
Q3	-.041	-.154	-.020	-.044	-.045	-.014	.035
	(-0.98)	(-0.38)	(-0.49)	(-1.06)	(-1.08)	(-0.34)	(0.86)
Q4	-.144	.010	.019	.010	-.002	.006	
	(-0.34)	(0.26)	(0.47)	(0.25)	(.041)	(0.14)	
P0212	-2.31						
	(-33.96)						
P0708	-1.63						
	(-24.02)						
P0712	-1.18						
	(-17.34)						
P0901	.627						
	(9.22)						
P3004	-1.27						
	(-18.67)						
P3310	-1.79						
	(-26.32)						
P3401	-1.52						
	(-22.43)						
P3403	-1.93						
	(-28.35)						
P3801	.896						
	(13.19)						
P3802	-.189						
	(-2.79)						

$R^2 = .966$ $R^2 = .967$ $R^2 = .966$ $R^2 = .966$ $R^2 = .964$ $R^2 = .966$ $R^2 = .966$

$F(15.182)$
$= 344$ $F = 352$ $F = 350$ $F = 348$ $F = 348$ $F = 349$ $F = 349$

Table 6.4. U.S. imports from Canada, 1996Q1 – 2005Q2

Variables	Model 1	Model 2	Model 3
Constant	8.84	9.28	9.55
	(9.49)	(10.13)	(10.17)
GDP	1.54	1.47	1.43
	(13.01)	(12.66)	(11.94)
Exchange rate	.002	.003	.004
	(0.94)	(1.84)	(2.24)
Q2	.030	.030	.029
	(1.83)	(1.83)	(1.77)
Q3	-.015	-.008	-.016
	(-0.84)	(-0.47)	(-0.96)
Q4	-.002	.003	.005
	(-0.13)	(0.15)	(0.28)
Yd01q3	-.100	-.103	-.086
	(-2.45)	(-2.54)	(-2.11)
Yd01q4	-.215	-.211	-.214
	(-5.30)	(-5.27)	(-5.35)
Yd02	-.194	-.198	-.194
	(-7.70)	(-7.95)	(-7.95)
Yd03	-.248	-.257	-.258
	(-9.09)	(-9.27)	(-9.40)
Yd04	-.168	-.166	-.175
	(-4.20)	(-4.52)	(-5.56)
Yd05	-.171	-.129	-.122
	(-3.05)	(-2.23)	(-2.24)
	R^2 = .987	R^2 = .988	R^2 = .988
	F = 1475	F = 1485	F = 1491

Table 6.5. Estimated import shortfalls, 2001Q3 – 2005Q2 (millions of USD)

Year/Qtr	Total
2001 Q3	5,170
2001 Q4	10,788
2002 Q1	9,980
2002 Q2	10,468
2002 Q3	10,155
2002 Q4	10,490
2003 Q1	13,252
2003 Q2	13,824
2003 Q3	13,478
2003 Q4	14,132
2004 Q1	10,098
2004 Q2	10,548
2004 Q3	10,342
2004 Q4	10,582
2005 Q1	11,035
2005 Q2	11,738

Table 6.6. U.S. exports to Canada, 1997Q1 – 2005Q2 models

Variables	Models 1	Models 2	Models 3	Models 4
Constant	14.30	15.27	16.12	16.38
	(12.18)	(13.14)	(13.70)	(13.66)
GDP	1.03	.907	.762	.754
	(5.79)	(4.96)	(3.91)	(3.77)
Exchange rate	.009	.008	.009	.007
	(4.91)	(4.18)	(3.52)	(3.51)
Q2	.051	.052	.048	.056
	(1.99)	(2.01)	(1.86)	(2.16)
Q3	-.015	-.021	-.033	-.026
	(-0.53)	(-0.75)	(-1.16)	(-0.93)
Q4	.028	.034	.024	.023
	(0.98)	(1.17)	(0.83)	(0.79)
Yd01q3	-.180	-.149	-.141	-.105
	(-2.90)	(2.43)	(-2.30)	(-1.73)
Yd01q4	-.228	-.218	-.206	-.191
	(-3.73)	(-3.53)	(-3.35)	(-3.13)
Yd02	-.198	-.177	-.177	-.152
	(-5.06)	(-4.57)	(-4.48)	(-4.07)
Yd03	-.158	-.174	-.187	-.190
	(-3.26)	(-3.53)	(-3.25)	(-3.77)
Yd04	-.039	-.031	.013	-.034
	(-0.52)	(-0.40)	(0.16)	(-0.42)
Yd05	.058	.051	.064	.045
	(0.53)	(0.45)	(0.55)	(0.38)
	R2 = .973	R2 = .972	R2 = .971	R2 = .971
	F = 613	F = 602	F = 598	F = 593

Table 6.7. Estimated export shortfalls, 2001Q3 – 2005Q2 (Millions of USD)

Year/Qtr	Total
2001 03	5,474
2001 04	8,156
2002 01	6,392
2002 02	6,985
2002 03	6,877
2002 04	7,103
2003 01	6,881
2003 02	7,702
2003 03	7,261
2003 04	7,197
2004 01	1,404
2004 02	1,424
2004 03	1,320
2004 04	1,514
2005 01	(2,556)
2005 02	(2,525)
Total	70,608

Figure 6.1. Aggregated U.S. imports from Canada (annualized; millions of USD)

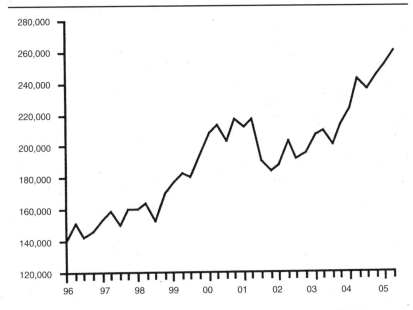

Figure 6.2. Aggregated U.S. exports to Canada (annualized; millions of USD)

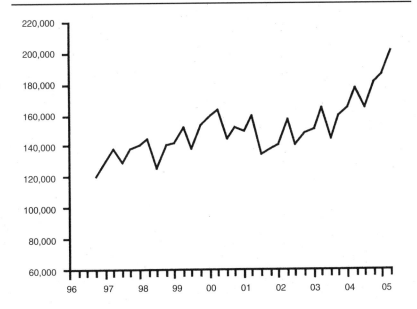

Table 7.1. U.S. imports from Canada, 1996Q1 – 2001Q2

Ports	Constant	GDP	Exchange rate	Q2	Q3	Q4	R2	F
1 Highgate Springs	20.11 (10.36)	.062 (0.24)	.001 (0.38) (1 quarter)	-.055 (-1.67)	-.062 (-1.79)	-.021 (-0.61)	.272	1.19
2 Alexandria Bay	7.83 (4.42)	1.28 (5.40)	.011 (3.12) (5 quarters)	.031 (0.90)	.052 (1.45)	.039 (1.09)	.921	37.45
3 Champlain–Rouses Point	8.06 (5.79)	1.39 (7.46)	.006 (2.04) (6 quarters)	.034 (1.31)	.027 (0.97)	.038 (1.35)	.941	50.91
4 Buffalo–Niagara Falls	18.83 (7.03)	.213 (0.59)	.014 (2.74) (contemporary)	.050 (1.12)	-.070 (-1.49)	-.027 (-0.57)	.744	9.31
5 Blaine	6.19 (5.00)	1.56 (9.40)	+.005 (1.88) (4 quarters)	.086 (3.57)	.083 (3.31)	.019 (0.75)	.958	72.01
6 Sweetgrass	5.92 (3.27)	1.35 (5.56)	.016 (4.48) (6 quarters)	.104 (3.06)	.055 (1.54)	.017 (0.48)	.947	56.83
7 Pembina	10.04 (3.68)	.818 (2.23)	.023 (4.16) (6 quarters)	-.029 (-0.56)	-.082 (-1.51)	-.049 (-0.90)	.876	22.50
8 Portal	7.70 (4.30)	1.33 (5.53)	.005 (1.44) (6 quarters)	.029 (0.85)	-.037 (-1.04)	.022 (0.62)	.898	28.12
9 Detroit	20.19 (20.44)	.199 (1.51)	.008 (3.91) (4 quarters)	.005 (0.24)	-.114 (-5.74)	-.025 (-1.27)	.883	24.19
10 Port Huron	5.23 (2.85)	1.71 (6.96)	.014 (3.72) (6 quarters)	.027 (0.77)	-.057 (-1.58)	.03 (0.83)	.952	63.53

Table 7.2. U.S. exports to Canada, 1997Q1 – 2001Q2

Ports	Constant	GDP	Exchange rate	Q2	Q3	Q4	R2	F
1 Highgate Springs	37.86 (7.88)	-3.89 (-2.16)	.051 (2.28) (current)	-.079 (-.32)	.002 (.01)	-.061 (-.23)	.734 (.208)	6.62
2 Alexandria Bay	9.98 (6.41)	1.39 (4.86)	.011 (3.10) (1 quarter)	.025 (.93)	.001 (.01)	-.003 (-.04)	.827 (.808)	11.44
3 Champlain–Rouses Point	17.74 (25.00)	.620 (4.84)	-.005 (-2.78) (current)	.040 (2.05)	-.038 (-1.82)	-.045 (-2.13)	.837 (.680)	6.62
4 Buffalo–Niagara Falls	15.35 (5.97)	1.16 (2.45)	.001 (.05) (current)	.052 (1.38)	-.087 (-2.21)	.055 (1.37)	.684 (.403)	5.20
5 Blaine	21.74 (22.76)	.018 (.102)	-.006 (-2.76) (current)	.072 (3.01)	.076 (3.02)	.044 (1.70)	.650 (.513)	4.46
6 Sweetgrass	4.01 (2.18)	2.83 (7.89)	-.013 (-3.14) (5 quarters)	-.029 (-.56)	-.094 (-1.72)	-.006 (-0.11)	.726 (.829)	6.37
7 Pembina	8.07 (3.30)	1.80 (3.73)	.007 (1.24) (6 quarters)	.087 (1.21)	-.023 (-0.30)	-.035 (-0.46)	.716 (.864)	6.06
8 Portal	5.26 (1.77)	2.67 (4.56)	-.016 (-2.43) (6 quarters)	.052 (1.02)	-.049 (-.92)	-.024 (-.44)	.422 (.628)	1.75
9 Detroit	18.77 (20.36)	.623 (3.67)	.003 (1.25) (1 quarter)	.016 (0.45)	-.133 (-3.53)	-.030 (-0.80)	.791 (.759)	9.07
10 Port Huron	13.12 (8.91)	.88 (3.26)	.022 (6.42) (1 quarter)	.059 (1.13)	.007 (0.13)	.031 (0.56)	.853 (.865)	13.94

Table 7.3. U.S. imports from Canada, 1996Q1 – 2005Q2

Variables					Ports					
	HS	AB	CR	B-NF	B1	SW	PM	PO	Det	PH
Constant	0.867	5.76	7.26	14.90	5.67	2.18	6.15	5.90	18.07	3.54
	(0.32)	(3.43)	(5.78)	(7.43)	(6.01)	(1.01)	(2.67)	(3.56)	(17.19)	(2.36)
GDP	2.53	1.60	1.53	.789	1.64	1.93	1.41	1.60	.515	1.98
	(7.19)	(7.56)	(9.56)	(3.11)	(13.71)	(6.98)	(4.82)	(7.58)	(3.87)	(10.36)
Exchange rate	-.006	.005	.003	.005	.003	.006	.012	.001	.002	.009
	(-1.38)	(1.81)	(1.38)	(1.54)	(1.97)	(1.58)	(3.13)	(0.14)	(1.28)	(3.44)
Q2	-.005	.046	.030	.047	.084	.070	-.007	.034	.023	.027
	(-0.10)	(1.56)	(1.38)	(1.38)	(5.07)	(1.89)	(-0.18)	(1.18)	(1.27)	(1.05)
Q3	-.038	.054	.009	-.044	.083	.013	-.070	-.012	-.077	-.069
	(-0.76)	(1.63)	(0.38)	(-1.19)	(4.64)	(0.32)	(-1.67)	(-0.39)	(-3.89)	(-2.49)
Q4	-.013	.025	-.003	-.008	.009	.007	-.028	.009	.007	.007
	(-0.25)	(0.77)	(-0.12)	(-0.02)	(0.47)	(0.18)	(-0.63)	(0.28)	(0.35)	(0.24)
Yd01q3	-.009	-.093	-.104	-.146	-.087	.065	-.041	-.024	-.117	-.079
	(-0.08)	(-1.25)	(-1.91)	(-1.73)	(-2.12)	(0.69)	(-0.41)	(-0.33)	(-2.56)	(-1.20)
Yd01q4	-.174	-.180	-.220	-.218	-.163	-.108	-.231	-.243	-.113	-.126
	(-1.56)	(-2.46)	(-4.14)	(-2.54)	(-3.96)	(-1.16)	(-2.36)	(-3.43)	(-2.47)	(-1.96)
Yd02	-.149	-.162	-.232	-.190	-.139	-.132	-.222	-.273	-.048	-.176
	(-2.16)	(-3.54)	(-7.08)	(-3.71)	(-5.42)	(-2.33)	(-3.70)	(-6.32)	(-1.67)	(-4.50)
Yd03	-.135	-.326	-.346	-.106	-.208	-.330	-.311	-.452	-.015	-.265
	(-1.59)	(-6.41)	(-9.42)	(-1.39)	(-7.48)	(-5.18)	(-4.61)	(-9.30)	(-0.48)	(-6.03)
Yd04	-.249	-.301	-.341	.026	-.110	-.191	-.230	-.267	.150	-.278
	(-1.67)	(-4.87)	(-8.08)	(0.22)	(-2.70)	(-2.62)	(-2.98)	(-4.80)	(3.32)	(-5.50)
Yd05	-.305	-.185	-.255	.023	-.132	-.207	-.058	-.208	.219	-.248
	(-1.42)	(-1.75)	(-3.48)	(0.15)	(-2.31)	(-1.63)	(-0.43)	(-2.15)	(3.45)	(-2.84)
R2	.912	.893	.915	.743	.974	.912	.868	.892	.939	.958
F	24.45	19.68	25.54	6.83	88.63	24.47	15.55	19.49	36.59	54.45

Table 7.4. U.S. exports to Canada 1997Q1 – 2005Q2

Variables		Ports									
	HS	AB	CR	B-NF	B1	SW	PM	PO	Det	PH
Constant	-4.42	7.47	17.25	25.66	18.70	11.14	8.61	16.06	18.68	11.59
	(-0.51)	(4.77)	(22.33)	(21.31)	(23.88)	(6.20)	(4.29)	(9.29)	(12.98)	(5.50)
GDP	2.46	1.69	.591	-.301	.389	1.57	1.77	.795	.619	1.25
	(1.87)	(7.13)	(5.05)	(-1.65)	(3.28)	(5.08)	(5.78)	(2.56)	(2.82)	(3.50)
Exchange rate	.056	.015	.001	-.006	-.002	-.006	.005	-.006	.033	.016
	(4.08)	(6.14)	(0.15)	(-2.93)	(-1.51)	(-1.84)	(1.42)	(-1.98)	(1.46)	(4.21)
Q2	.055	.037	.037	.049	.087	-.044	.089	.049	.044	.084
	(0.29)	(1.10)	(2.23)	(1.89)	(5.11)	(-1.18)	(2.04)	(1.54)	(1.39)	(1.83)
Q3	.106	-.004	-.061	-.064	.079	-.142	-.041	-.055	-.134	-.005
	(0.51)	(-0.70)	(-3.28)	(-2.20)	(4.20)	(-3.32)	(-0.86)	(-1.55)	(-3.91)	(-0.10)
Q4	.274	-.011	-.049	.044	.062	-.058	-.054	-.015	-.013	.048
	(1.28)	(-0.30)	(-2.58)	(1.49)	(3.23)	(-1.34)	(-1.09)	(-0.38)	(-0.37)	(0.92)
Yd01q3	-1.10	-.243	-.073	-.102	-.044	.109	-.122	.047	-.029	-.179
	(-2.42)	(-2.94)	(-1.80)	(-1.60)	(-1.07)	(1.26)	(-1.16)	(0.63)	(-0.38)	(-1.62)
Yd01q4	-1.57	-.230	-.128	-.044	-.149	.065	-.121	.060	-.057	-.216
	(-3.37)	(-2.82)	(-3.18)	(-3.41)	(-3.66)	(0.76)	(-1.12)	(0.81)	(-0.73)	(-1.91)
Yd02	-.896	-.250	-.154	-.293	-.147	-.036	-.132	.009	.107	-.023
	(-3.20)	(-4.79)	(-5.98)	(-7.29)	(-5.63)	(-0.65)	(-2.03)	(0.21)	(2.30)	(-1.07)
Yd03	-.226	-.345	-.237	-.189	-.105	-.131	-.154	.123	.048	.200
	(-0.60)	(-5.31)	(-7.40)	(-3.79)	(-3.22)	(-1.84)	(-1.76)	(2.01)	(0.77)	(2.18)
Yd04	.286	-.271	-.201	-.072	-.007	-.290	-.227	.179	.054	.208
	(0.48)	(-2.65)	(-3.95)	(-0.92)	(-0.15)	(-2.50)	(-1.66)	(1.72)	(0.55)	(1.44)
Yd05	.752	-.251	-.154	-.094	.019	-.406	-.265	.204	.143	.163
	(0.91)	(-1.72)	(2.14)	(-0.83)	(0.26)	(-2.15)	(-1.39)	(1.12)	(1.05)	(0.81)
R2	.591	.853	.892	.918	.932	.856	.872	.932	.876	.876
F	2.89	11.61	16.55	22.42	27.35	11.85	13.64	27.49	14.17	14.18

Table 8.1. Market share for foreign vehicles made in North America (units sold)

	Passenger cars (%)	Trucks (%)
1995	18.8	2.1
2000	24.2	6.4
2003	29.3	8.7
First 9 months – 2004	30.9	9.2

Source: Statistics Canada (2004), 'New Motor Vehicle Sales,' *The Daily*, September, www.statcan.ca/daily/English/04115/d041115b.htm

Table 8.2. U.S. intra-industry trade index in autos by NAICs subsector

Subsector	Partner	1997	2004
3361 Assembly	Canada	0.57	0.56
	Mexico	0.28	0.36
3362 Bodies	Canada	0.71	0.81
	Mexico	0.53	0.64
3363 Parts	Canada	0.70	0.82
	Mexico	0.88	0.51

Source: Hufbauer and Schott (2005)

Table 10.1. Inward and outward FDI to GDP (percentage)

	Canada		United States	
June period	Inward FDI/GDP	Outward FDI/GDP	Inward FDI/GDP	Outward FDI/GDP
1990–1995	1.06	1.15	0.63	0.97
1995–2000	3.04	3.12	1.96	1.58
2001–2005	1.88	3.30	1.01	1.27

Source: OECD (2006a, b)

Table 10.2. Canadian outward FDI (stocks) to the world (percentage)

	1990	2001	2002	2003	2004
United States	61	51	46	41	43
Other	39	49	54	59	57

Source: Asia Pacific Foundation, 'Canadian Outward Foreign Direct Investment to the World,' www.asiapacificbusiness.ca/data/trade/general_dataset5_toworld.cfm

Table 10.3. Growth in real total domestic demand (percentage change)

	1990	2000	2001	2002	2003	2004	2005
Canada	4.2	4.0	3.2	3.1	3.6	3.7	4.5
United States	5.3	4.4	0.9	2.2	3.0	4.7	3.6

Source: International Monetary Fund, Public Information Notices, 29 March 2005; 28 July 2006 (mimeo) and RBC Financial Group, Economic and Financial Market Outlook, March 2006 (mimeo)

Table 10.4. Gross fixed (private) domestic investment (percentage change)

	1990	2000	2001	2002	2003	2004	2005
Canada	6.2	4.8	3.3	1.4	4.6	6.0	7.2
United States	8.3	6.5	-3.0	-5.2	3.6	9.7	8.1

Sources: Same as Table 10.3

Appendix A
U.S. Exports and Imports by Port
(Millions of USD)

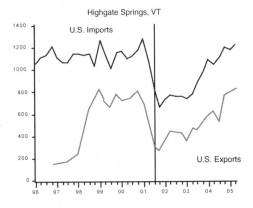

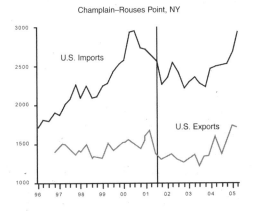

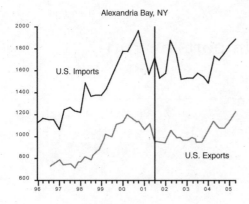

Alexandria Bay, NY

Buffalo–Niagara Falls, NY

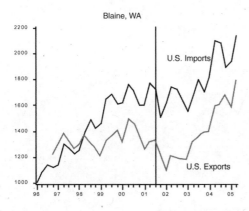

Blaine, WA

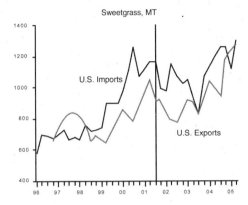

Sweetgrass, MT

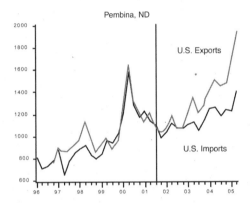

Pembina, ND

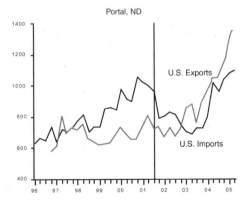

Portal, ND

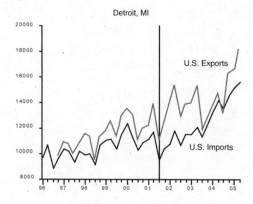

Detroit, MI

Port Huron, MI

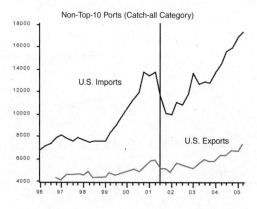

Non-Top-10 Ports (Catch-all Category)

Appendix B
Imports from and Exports to Canada: Share of Value of the Ten Largest Commodities (in per cent)

Alexandria Bay, NY – Imports from Canada

SITC2 Description	2001Q2	SITC2 Description	2005Q2
68 Nonferrous metals	22.4	68 Nonferrous metals	21.9
64 Paper, paperboard	22.2	97 Gold, nonmonetary	16.8
97 Gold, nonmonetary	12.2	64 Paper, paperboard	13.6
65 Textile yarn, fabrics	8.2	54 Medicinal and pharmaceutical	11.9
93 Special transactions	7.8	78 Road vehicles	10.9
78 Road vehicles	7.6	65 Textile yarn, fabrics	7.4
89 Miscellaneous manufactured	5.3	93 Special transactions	5.1
76 Telecommunications	5.1	89 Miscellaneous manufactured	4.9
69 Manufactures of metals, N.E.S	4.6	77 Electrical machinery	3.8
82 Furniture and parts	4.6	82 Furniture and parts	3.7

Alexandria Bay, NY – Exports to Canada

SITC2 Description	2001Q2	SITC2 Description	2005Q2
68 Nonferrous metals	18.6	68 Nonferrous metals	25.6
65 Textile yarn, fabrics	13.5	78 Road vehicles	12.4
76 Telecommunications	13.3	64 Paper, paperboard	11.3
78 Road vehicles	11.6	65 Textile yarn, fabrics	11.3
64 Paper, paperboard	10.8	72 Machinery specialized	7.6
77 Electrical machinery	7.5	71 Power generating machinery	7.1
93 Special transactions	7.1	57 Plastics in primary forms	7.0
74 General industrial machinery	6.1	77 Electrical machinery	6.0
89 Miscellaneous manufactured	5.8	89 Miscellaneous manufactured	5.9
57 Plastics in primary forms	5.7	74 General industrial machinery	5.7

Highgate Springs, VT – Imports from Canada

SITC2 Description	2001Q2	SITC2 Description	2005Q2
77 Electrical machinery	54.6	77 Electrical machinery	44.8
64 Paper, paperboard	7.6	93 Special transactions	18.5
93 Special transactions	6.6	64 Paper, paperboard	7.2
84 Articles of apparel and clothing	5.9	71 Power generating machinery	6.4
24 Cork and wood	5.6	84 Articles of apparel and clothing	4.9
68 Nonferrous metals	5.3	68 Nonferrous metals	4.7
71 Power generating machinery	4.6	63 Cork and wood manufactures	3.4
89 Miscellaneous manufactured	4.0	24 Cork and wood	3.4
74 General industrial machinery	3.1	75 Office machines	3.4
63 Cork and wood manufactures	2.7	89 Miscellaneous manufactured	3.4

Highgate Springs, VT – Exports to Canada

SITC2 Description	2001Q2	SITC2 Description	2005Q2
77 Electrical machinery	67.8	77 Electrical machinery	76.7
93 Special transactions	8.0	71 Power generating machinery	10.3
71 Power generating machinery	6.2	74 General industrial machinery	2.7
64 Paper, paperboard	3.9	28 Metalliferous ores and metal	2.5
69 Manufactures of metals	3.2	64 Paper, paperboard	2.3
89 Miscellaneous manufactured	2.8	89 Miscellaneous manufactured	1.6
72 Machinery specialized	2.4	78 Road vehicles	1.3
65 Textile yarn, fabrics	2.2	65 Textile yarn, fabrics	1.0
74 General industrial machinery	2.0	75 Office machines	0.9
28 Metalliferous ores and metal	1.5	57 Plastics in primary forms	0.8

Buffalo–Niagara Falls, NY – Imports from Canada

SITC2	Description	2001Q2	SITC2	Description	2005Q2
78	Road vehicles	47.7	78	Road vehicles	41.0
34	Gas, natural and manufactured	9.8	34	Gas, natural and manufactured	15.5
93	Special transactions	7.8	68	Nonferrous metals	7.2
74	General industrial machinery	6.0	89	Miscellaneous manufactured	7.0
68	Nonferrous metals	5.9	74	General industrial machinery	6.9
89	Miscellaneous manufactured	5.8	93	Special transactions	5.6
64	Paper, paperboard	4.7	82	Furniture and parts	4.8
71	Power generating machinery	4.2	64	Paper, paperboard	4.6
82	Furniture and parts	4.1	69	Manufactures of metals, N.E.S	3.8
77	Electrical machinery	4.1	33	Petroleum, petroleum products	3.7

Buffalo–Niagara Falls, NY – Exports to Canada

SITC2	Description	2001Q2	SITC2	Description	2005Q2
78	Road vehicles	36.1	78	Road vehicles	28.7
89	Miscellaneous manufactured	9.4	89	Miscellaneous manufactured	11.9
74	General industrial machinery	9.2	34	Gas, natural and manufactured	10.5
77	Electrical machinery	9.1	74	General industrial machinery	9.8
71	Power generating machinery	8.7	77	Electrical machinery	8.0
75	Office machines and automatic	8.1	67	Iron and steel	7.3
69	Manufactures of metals, N.E.S	5.4	75	Office machines	7.1
64	Paper, paperboard	4.8	71	Power generating machinery	5.8
76	Telecommunications	4.7	55	Essential oils and resinoids	5.5
72	Machinery specialized	4.4	64	Paper, paperboard	5.3

Champlain–Rouses Point, NY – Imports from Canada

SITC2 Description	2001Q2	SITC2 Description	2005Q2
93 Special transactions	16.8	64 Paper, paperboard	16.7
64 Paper, paperboard	15.0	68 Nonferrous metals	15.2
78 Road vehicles	11.2	35 Electric current	10.3
35 Electric current	11.0	89 Miscellaneous manufactured	9.8
84 Articles of apparel and clothing	10.3	93 Special transactions	9.4
89 Miscellaneous manufactured	9.2	63 Cork and wood manufactures	8.9
79 Transport equipment	7.7	79 Transport equipment, N.E.S.	8.4
82 Furniture and parts	7.4	84 Articles of apparel and clothing	7.5
24 Cork and wood	6.0	24 Cork and wood	7.3
68 Nonferrous metals	5.3	78 Road vehicles	6.5

Champlain–Rouses Point, NY – Exports to Canada

SITC2 Description	2001Q2	SITC2 Description	2005Q2
71 Power generating machinery	23.9	54 Medicinal and pharmaceutical	20.9
78 Road vehicles	11.4	78 Road vehicles	13.4
54 Medicinal and pharmaceutical	10.1	05 Vegetables and fruit	10.1
65 Textile yarn, fabrics	9.8	72 Machinery specialized	9.7
77 Electrical machinery	8.9	77 Electrical machinery	9.0
74 General industrial machinery	7.4	89 Miscellaneous manufactured	8.4
79 Transport equipment	7.3	74 General industrial machinery	7.6
72 Machinery specialized	7.1	65 Textile yarn, fabrics	7.5
5 Vegetables and fruit	7.0	71 Power generating machinery	7.2
89 Miscellaneous manufactured	7.0	64 Paper, paperboard	6.2

Blaine, WA – Imports from Canada

SITC2 Description	2001Q2	SITC2 Description	2005Q2
24 Cork and wood	19.5	24 Cork and wood	21.5
93 Special transactions	17.1	63 Cork and wood manufactures	20.3
64 Paper, paperboard	14.0	64 Paper, paperboard	13.0
63 Cork and wood manufactures	10.8	93 Special transactions	11.5
3 Fish (not marine mammals)	8.8	89 Miscellaneous manufactured	7.5
79 Transport equipment, N.E.S.	7.7	03 Fish (not marine mammals)	7.3
89 Miscellaneous manufactured	6.8	69 Manufactures of metals, N.E.S.	5.5
78 Road vehicles	5.9	05 Vegetables and fruit	4.7
69 Manufactures of metals, N.E.S.	4.8	78 Road vehicles	4.5
05 Vegetables and fruit	4.6	51 Organic chemicals	4.3

Blaine, WA – Exports to Canada

SITC2 Description	2001Q2	SITC2 Description	2005Q2
89 Miscellaneous manufactured	14.4	78 Road vehicles	17.7
05 Vegetables and fruit	13.6	05 Vegetables and fruit	14.4
72 Machinery specialized	11.4	89 Miscellaneous manufactured	12.0
74 General industrial machinery	10.4	74 General industrial machinery	10.7
78 Road vehicles	9.5	75 Office machines	9.4
64 Paper, paperboard	9.1	72 Machinery specialized	8.8
75 Office machines	8.8	77 Electrical machinery	7.5
77 Electrical machinery	8.1	64 Paper, paperboard	7.1
76 Telecommunications	7.6	69 Manufactures of metals, N.E.S.	6.5
69 Manufactures of metals, N.E.S.	7.1	67 Iron and steel	5.9

Sweetgrass, MT – Imports from Canada

SITC2 Description	2001Q2	SITC2 Description	2005Q2
01 Meat and meat preparations	21.1	01 Meat and meat preparations	27.2
93 Special transactions	18.2	33 Petroleum, petroleum products	26.4
33 Petroleum, petroleum products	15.9	93 Special transactions	15.0
00 Live animals other than fish	10.7	74 General industrial machinery	7.0
76 Telecommunications	9.9	72 Machinery specialized	5.3
78 Road vehicles	6.4	63 Cork and wood manufactures	4.7
35 Electric current	6.4	56 Fertilizers	4.6
74 General industrial machinery	5.6	78 Road vehicles	3.9
72 Machinery specialized	3.2	69 Manufactures of metals, N.E.S.	3.0
24 Cork and wood	2.6	76 Telecommunications	2.7

Sweetgrass, MT – Exports to Canada

SITC2 Description	2001Q2	SITC2 Description	2005Q2
74 General industrial machinery	21.4	78 Road vehicles	19.5
71 Power generating machinery	16.7	74 General industrial machinery	18.1
79 Transport equipment, N.E.S.	12.2	72 Machinery specialized	14.7
72 Machinery specialized	9.9	05 Vegetables and fruit	10.6
78 Road vehicles	8.9	34 Gas, natural and manufactured	9.3
05 Vegetables and fruit	8.3	75 Office machines	8.6
59 Chemical materials and product	6.0	67 Iron and steel	5.7
76 Telecommunications	5.9	69 Manufactures of metals, N.E.S.	4.8
77 Electrical machinery	5.7	59 Chemical materials	4.5
69 Manufactures of metals, N.E.S.	5.0	89 Miscellaneous manufactured	4.2

Pembina, ND – Imports from Canada

SITC2 Description	2001Q2	SITC2 Description	2005Q2
78 Road vehicles	16.7	78 Road vehicles	17.4
35 Electric current	14.4	93 Special transactions	14.5
93 Special transactions	12.2	72 Machinery specialized	11.1
00 Live animals other than fish	12.0	00 Live animals other than fish,	9.6
01 Meat and meat preparations	8.1	01 Meat and meat preparations	8.6
82 Furniture and parts	7.7	74 General industrial machinery	8.5
72 Machinery specialized	7.7	89 Miscellaneous manufactured	8.5
74 General industrial machinery	7.1	82 Furniture and parts	7.7
64 Paper, paperboard	7.1	35 Electric current	7.4
76 Telecommunications	7.1	64 Paper, paperboard	6.6

Pembina, ND – Exports to Canada

SITC2 Description	2001Q2	SITC2 Description	2005Q2
72 Machinery	20.1	72 Machinery specialized	22.9
78 Road vehicles	17.3	78 Road vehicles	18.0
74 General industrial machinery	16.0	74 General industrial machinery	16.2
59 Chemical materials	10.1	89 Miscellaneous manufactured	9.1
89 Miscellaneous manufactured	9.5	59 Chemical materials	7.6
71 Power generating machinery	8.2	71 Power generating machinery	6.9
77 Electrical machinery	5.4	77 Electrical machinery	6.2
69 Manufactures of metals, N.E.S.	4.9	69 Manufactures of metals, N.E.S.	5.0
64 Paper, paperboard	4.6	67 Iron and steel	5.0
65 Textile yarn, fabrics	4.0	64 Paper, paperboard	3.2

Portal, ND – Imports from Canada

SITC2 Description	2001Q2	SITC2 Description	2005Q2
76 Telecommunications	23.3	24 Cork and wood	22.1
24 Cork and wood	21.6	57 Plastics in primary forms	21.1
51 Organic chemicals	13.0	52 Inorganic chemicals	12.5
57 Plastics in primary forms	11.1	56 Fertilizers	9.2
52 Inorganic chemicals	6.8	51 Organic chemicals	7.0
56 Fertilizers	5.5	93 Special transactions	6.3
93 Special transactions	5.5	72 Machinery specialized	6.0
64 Paper, paperboard	4.8	25 Pulp and waste paper	5.5
78 Road vehicles	4.4	32 Coal, coke and briquettes	5.2
00 Live animals other than fish	4.1	63 Cork and wood manufactures	5.1

Portal, ND – Exports to Canada

SITC2 Description	2001Q2	SITC2 Description	2005Q2
72 Machinery specialized	20.3	78 Road vehicles	26.1
78 Road vehicles	20.3	72 Machinery specialized	21.6
59 Chemical materials and product	13.9	74 General industrial machinery	12.5
74 General industrial machinery	11.8	67 Iron and steel	11.8
71 Power generating machinery	7.1	71 Power generating machinery	7.1
67 Iron and steel	6.8	59 Chemical materials	6.7
77 Electrical machinery	6.7	77 Electrical machinery	4.1
79 Transport equipment, N.E.S.	6.3	51 Organic chemicals	3.6
88 Photographic apparatus	3.4	57 Plastics in primary forms	3.4
89 Miscellaneous manufactured	3.4	69 Manufactures of metals, N.E.S.	3.1

Detroit, MI – Imports from Canada

SITC2 Description	2001Q2	SITC2 Description	2005Q2
78 Road vehicles	63.3	78 Road vehicles	67.3
71 Power generating machinery	7.7	71 Power generating machinery	7.2
74 General industrial machinery	5.7	74 General industrial machinery	5.5
69 Manufactures of metals, N.E.S.	4.0	69 Manufactures of metals, N.E.S.	3.9
93 Special transactions	4.0	82 Furniture and parts	3.2
82 Furniture and parts	3.7	89 Miscellaneous manufactured	2.8
64 Paper, paperboard	3.6	67 Iron and steel	2.6
89 Miscellaneous manufactured	2.8	64 Paper, paperboard	2.6
77 Electrical machinery	2.7	62 Rubber manufactures, N.E.S.	2.5
62 Rubber manufactures, N.E.S.	2.5	93 Special transactions	2.5

Detroit, MI – Exports to Canada

SITC2 Description	2001Q2	SITC2 Description	2005Q2
78 Road vehicles	48.1	78 Road vehicles	52.9
71 Power generating machinery	11.9	71 Power generating machinery	11.8
74 General industrial machinery	8.9	74 General industrial machinery	7.2
77 Electrical machinery	7.6	77 Electrical machinery	6.3
75 Office machines	4.6	75 Office machines	5.3
69 Manufactures of metals, N.E.S.	4.6	89 Miscellaneous manufactured	3.8
89 Miscellaneous manufactured	4.3	76 Telecommunications	3.3
76 Telecommunications	3.6	69 Manufactures of metals, N.E.S.	3.3
87 Profssional, scientific	3.6	87 Profssional, scientific	3.1
82 Furniture and parts	2.9	67 Iron and steel	3.0

Port Huron, MI – Imports from Canada

SITC2 Description	2001Q2	SITC2 Description	2005Q2
78 Road vehicles	59.0	78 Road vehicles	47.0
34 Gas, natural and manufactured	6.8	34 Gas, natural and manufactured	11.7
68 Nonferrous metals	6.5	68 Nonferrous metals	10.5
64 Paper, paperboard	5.7	33 Petroleum, petroleum products	6.1
93 Special transactions	5.1	64 Paper, paperboard	6.1
71 Power generating machinery	4.0	57 Plastics in primary forms	4.6
33 Petroleum, petroleum products	3.9	74 General industrial machinery	3.8
57 Plastics in primary forms	3.7	71 Power generating machinery	3.6
74 General industrial machinery	3.1	93 Special transactions	3.4
82 Furniture and parts	2.3	82 Furniture and parts	3.2

Port Huron, MI – Exports to Canada

SITC2 Description	2001Q2	SITC2 Description	2005Q2
78 Road vehicles	33.8	78 Road vehicles	24.8
71 Power generating machinery	12.3	57 Plastics in primary forms	11.1
74 General industrial machinery	9.9	34 Gas, natural and manufactured	10.1
57 Plastics in primary forms	7.4	74 General industrial machinery	9.9
77 Electrical machinery	7.3	89 Miscellaneous manufactured	9.0
72 Machinery specialized	6.8	51 Organic chemicals	8.8
51 Organic chemicals	6.4	72 Machinery specialized	8.5
89 Miscellaneous manufactured	6.2	77 Electrical machinery	7.1
69 Manufactures of metals, N.E.S.	5.4	76 Telecommunications	5.3
59 Chemical materials	4.5	69 Manufactures of metals, N.E.S.	5.3

Appendix C
Truck Share of Truck Plus Rail Shipments

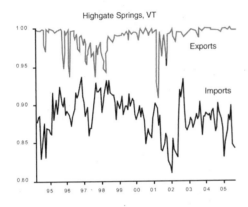

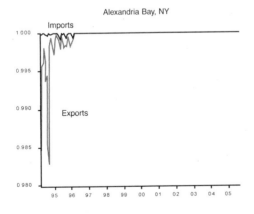

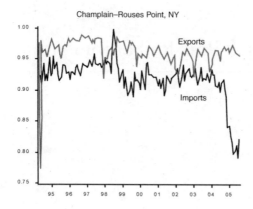

Champlain–Rouses Point, NY

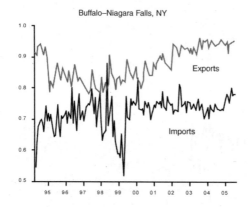

Buffalo–Niagara Falls, NY

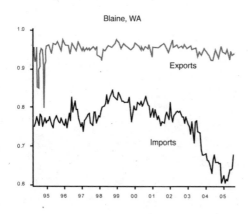

Blaine, WA

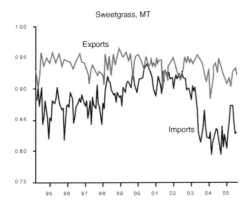

Sweetgrass, MT

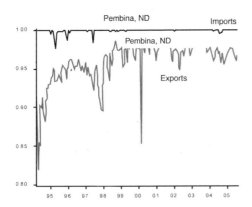

Pembina, ND

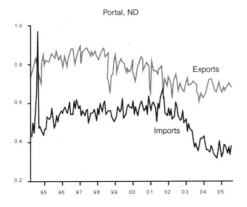

Portal, ND

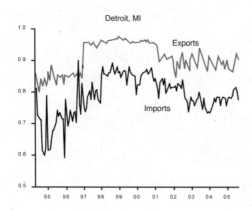

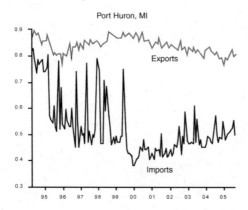

References

9/11 Commission. 2004. *Final Report of the National Commission on Terrorist Attacks upon the United States*. New York: W.W. Norton.

Andreas, Peter. 2003. 'A Tale of Two Borders: The U.S.–Canada and U.S.–Mexico Lines after 9/11.' In Peter Andreas and Thomas J. Biersteker, eds., *The Rebordering of North America*, 1–23. New York: Routledge.

Auto Channel. 2005. 'Ward's Reports Estimated Weekly North American Vehicle Production.' www.theautochannel.com/news/2005/10/21/146155.html.

Battelle. 2003. 'Further Assessment of the FY 2001 International Border Measurement Project.' Report Prepared for the Office of Freight Management and Operations, Federal Highway Administration, Columbus, OH. Mimeo.

Belelieu, Andre. 2003. 'The Smart Border Process at Two: Losing Momentum?' *Hemisphere Focus* 11(31): 1–11.

Belzer, Michael. 2004. 'The Jobs Tunnel: The Economic Impact of Adequate Border Crossing Infrastructure.' Mimeo.

Bissett, John. 2003. 'Troubled Borders: Canada, the U.S.A., and Mexico.' Presentation to the Trilateral Commission, New York, 14–16 November.

Block, Robert. 2006. 'White House Seeks Big Increase for Border Security.' *Wall Street Journal*, 7 February, A18.

Bonsor, Norman. 2004. 'Fixing the Potholes in North American Transportation Systems.' *Choices* 10(8): 1–18.

Brooks, Rick. 2003. 'Shippers Say New Border Rules Could Delay Just-in-Time Cargo.' *The Wall Street Journal*, 29 August, 1.

Center for Automotive Research. 2002. The Canada–U.S. Border: An Automotive Case Study.' Ann Arbor: Altarum Institute. Mimeo.

Coalition for Secure and Trade-Efficient Borders. 2005. 'Rethinking our Borders: A New North American Partnership.' Montreal. Mimeo.

Collins, Michelle. 2002. 'Canada Ranks First in North American Automotive Productivity.' *CanadaOne Magazine*. www.canadaone.com/ezine/sept02/automotive_productivity.html.

Combes, Pierre-Philippe, Miren Lafourcade, and Thierry Mayer. 2003. 'Can Business and Social Networks Explain the Border Effect Puzzle?' Paris: CEPII. Mimeo.

Courchene, Thomas, and Richard Harris. 1999. *From Fixing to Monetary Union: Options for North American Currency Integration*. Toronto: C.D. Howe Institute.

DAMF Consulting. 2005. 'The Economic Impact of Post-September 11, 2001, U.S. Border Security Measures on the Canadian Trucking Industry.' Mimeo.

deGroot, Henri, Gert-Jan Linders, Piet Rietveld, and Uma Subramanian. 2004. 'The Institutional Determinants of Bilateral Trade Patterns.' *Kyklos* 57(1): 103–23.

Ferrabee, James. 2006. 'No Choice but to Reform Our Immigration Laws.' *Toronto Star*, 6 May, F5.

Ferley, Paul. 2004. 'Canadian Export Growth – Gauging the Impact of the Stronger Dollar.' Toronto: Bank of Montreal. Mimeo.

Flynn, Stephen. 2003. 'The False Conundrum.' In Peter Andreas and Thomas J. Biersteker, eds., *The Rebordering of North America*, 110–27. New York: Routledge.

Frankel, Jeffrey, and Andrew Rose. 2002. 'An Estimate of the Effects of Common Currencies on Trade and Income.' *Quarterly Journal of Economics* (May): 437–66.

deGroot, Henri, Gert-Jan Linders, Piet Rietveld, and Uma Subramanian. 2004. The Institutional Determinants of Bilateral Trade Flows. *Kyklos* 51(1): 103–24.

Globerman, Steven. 2005. 'Border Security and Canada's Economic Future.' Revision of a paper prepared for NAFTA@10 Workshop, Ottawa, 4–6 February 2005. Bellingham, Western Washington University. Mimeo.

Globerman, Steven, and Daniel Shapiro. 1999. 'The Impact of Government Policies on Foreign Direct Investment: The Canadian Experience.' *Journal of International Business Studies* 30(3): 513–32.

– 2002. 'Global Foreign Direct Investment Flows.' *World Development* 30(11): 1899–1919.

– 2003. 'Assessing Recent Patterns of Foreign Direct Investment in Canada and the United States.' In Richard Harris, ed., *North American Linkages: Opportunities and Challenges*, 279–308. Calgary: University of Calgary Press.

Globerman, Steven, and Paul Storer. 2004. Canada–U.S. Economic Integration following NAFTA.' In Alan Rugman, ed., *North American Economic and Financial Integration*, 17–46. Amsterdam: Elsevier.

– 2005. 'Canada–U.S. Free Trade and Price Convergence in North America.' *American Review of Canadian Studies* (Autumn): 423–52.

Goldfarb, Danielle. 2005. 'The Linkages between Border Security and Economic Integration.' Paper presented at Conference on Border Security and Canada–U.S. Integration: Toward a Research Policy Agenda Conference. Border Policy Research Institute, Bellingham, WA, 26 April.

Goldfarb, Danielle, and William Robson. 2003. 'Risky Business: U.S. Border Security and the Threat to Canadian Exports.' Toronto: C.D. Howe Commentary, No. 177.

Gould, D. 1994. 'Immigrant Links to Home Country: Empirical Implications for U.S. Bilateral Trade Flows.' *Review of Economics and Statistics* 76: 302–16.

Government of British Columbia. 2005. BC Stats-Exports. www.bcstats .gov.bc.ca.

Government of Canada. 2004. 'CEO's Guide to World Business Costs – Automotive.' Ottawa.

Hejazi, Walid, and A. Edward Safarian. 1999. 'Trade, Foreign Direct Investment, and R&D Spillovers.' *Journal of International Business Studies* 30(3): 491–512.

Hufbauer, Gary, and Jeffrey Schott. 2005. *NAFTA Revisited: Achievements and Challenges*. Washington, DC: Institute for International Economics.

Koring, Paul. 2006. Canadian Catch Leads to American Anxiety. *Globe and Mail*, 5 June, A3.

Krugman, Paul. 1991. *Geography and Trade*. Cambridge, MA: MIT Press.

Kudrle, Robert. 1995. 'Canada's Foreign Investment Review Agency and United States Direct Investment in Canada.' *Transnational Corporations* 4(2): 58–91.

Lee, Linda, Pierre Martin, Estelle Ouellet, and Francois Vaillancourt. 2005. 'American Border Security Measures: Potential Economic Impacts and Policy Responses from a Quebec Perspective.' Montreal: University of Montreal. Mimeo.

MacPherson, Alan, and James McConnell. 2005. 'The Economic Impacts of U.S. Government Antiterrorism Policies and Regulations on Cross-Border Commerce between Southern Ontario and Western New York.' Buffalo: Canada–U.S. Trade Center, State University of New York at Buffalo. Mimeo.

McLellan, Anne. 2005. Comments on the Review of Bill C-26, Subcommittee on Public Safety and National Security, Ottawa, 1 February, 2005. www.parl .gc.ca/infocomdoc/38/1/SNSN/Meetings/Evidence/SNSNEV03-E.pdf.

Meyers, Deborah Waller. 2003. 'Does Smarter Lead to Safer? An Assessment of the Border Accords with Canada and Mexico.' Washington, DC: Migration Policy Institute. Mimeo.

– 2005. *One Face at the Border: Beyond the Slogan*. Washington, DC: Migration Policy Institute. Mimeo.

Natural Resources Canada. 2004. 'Annual Economic Review and Outlook for the Canadian Forest Sector: 2004–5.' www.nrcan-rncan.gc.ca/cfs-scf/national/What-quoi/pub_annualeconrev_e.html.

OECD (Organization for Economic Co-operation and Development). 2006a. *OECD Factbook: Economic Environmental and Social Statistics*. Paris.

– 2006b). *Trends and Recent Developments in Foreign Direct Investment*. Paris. Mimeo.

Ontario Chamber of Commerce. 2004. 'Cost of Border Delays in Ontario.' Toronto. Mimeo (May).

Perimeter Clearance Coalition. 2002. *Perimeter Clearance Strategy*. Bound report.

Random Lengths. 2005. 'U.S.–Canada Trade Dispute Timeline.' Eugene: Random Lengths. Mimeo.

Rauch, J. 2001. 'Business and Social Networks in International Trade.' *Journal of Economic Literature* 39: 1177–203.

Rosenthal, Stuart S., and William C. Strange. 2003. 'Geography, Industrial Organization, and Agglomeration.' *Review of Economics and Statistics* 85(2): 377–93.

Snodgrass, Coral, Guy Gessner, and John Occhipinti. 2004. 'Check Points or Choke Points: The Impact of New Security Measures on U.S.–Canadian Trade Relations.' Buffalo: Canisius College. Mimeo.

Security and Prosperity Partnership. 2005a. Joint Statement of President Bush, President Fox, and Prime Minister Martin, March 2005. www.whitehouse.gov/news/releases/2005/03/20050323-2.html

– 2005b. *Report to Leaders*, June 2005. www.spp.gov/report_to_leaders/Trilingual_Report_to_Leaders.pdf.

Senate Committee on National Security and Defence. 2005. *Borderline Insecure*. Interim Report issued June 2005. www.parl.gc.ca/38/1/parlbus/commbus/senate/com-e/defe-e/rep-e/repintjun05-e.pdf.

Studer, Isabel. 2004. 'The North American Auto Industry.' IRPP Working Paper Series No. 2004-09o. Montreal: Institute for Research on Public Policy.

Taylor, John, Douglas Robideaux, and George Jackson. 2003. 'The U.S.–Canada Border: Cost Impacts, Causes, and Short to Long Term Management Options.' Allendale, Michigan, Grand Valley State University. Mimeo.

U.S. Department of Transportation. 2002. 'Commercial Vehicle Travel Time and Delay at U.S. Border Crossings.' Washington, DC: Office of Freight Management and Operations. Mimeo.

Webber, Joel. 2005. Canada–U.S. Freight Security: The Next Level.' *Fraser Forum* (March): 13–14.

Index